The NVQ *and* GNVQ
Assessor
Handbook

**A Practical
Guide to
Units D32, D33,
D34 and D36**

D1388454

Ros Ollin and
Jenny Tucker

KOGAN
PAGE

First published in 1994
Reprinted with minor revisions 1995
Reprinted 1995

Kogan Page Limited
120 Pentonville Road
London N1 9JN

British Library Cataloguing in Publication Data

A CIP record for this book is available from the British Library

ISBN 0 7494 1356 5

Typeset by Books Unlimited (Nottm), Rainworth, NG21 0JE
Printed and bound in Great Britain by
Biddles Ltd, Guildford and King's Lynn

Contents

SECTION 2

SECTION 3

SECTION 4

Acknowledgements

We would like to acknowledge the help and support of Roy and Dorothy Ollin, Luke and Jessie Blindell and the Roe family, especially Phil Roe, who allowed his dining room to be turned into a study. Equally, thanks to Bill and Rosina Fitch and Jeremy Tucker for their very practical support in word-processing.

Our sincere thanks to all friends, colleagues and candidates, too numerous to mention, who have directly and indirectly contributed to the writing of this book, in particular to Andrew Milner, for his help with the graphics and proof-reading.

Foreword

The revolution in vocational qualifications in Britain is now gathering pace. The development of National Vocational Qualifications (NVQs) in the workplace and the introduction of General National Vocational Qualifications (GNVQs) in schools and colleges are key components of achieving a learning society which can be competitive in the global marketplace.

If this revolution is to transform the British economy and the lives of its citizens, thousands upon thousands of supervisors, managers, teachers and many others will need to assess the competence and learning outcomes of all of us who wish to demonstrate we have reached the standards which underpin NVQs and GNVQs. This process of assessment, and verification of the assessment process, is at the heart of this revolution of British qualifications and, unless it is a quality process, then NVQs and GNVQs will be devalued as qualifications.

This is why assessors and verifiers need to be trained to the standards laid down by the Training and Development Lead Body, which I have chaired since it was formed in 1989. Those standards have recently been revised as part of a major review of all standards produced by the TDLB and I am immensely grateful to Roy Harrison of the Confederation of British Industry for his hard work in chairing the review group which had responsibility for overseeing this revision. He and his colleagues on the review group have done an outstanding job.

It gives me particular pleasure to welcome this guide to the TDLB units for assessors and verifiers as it has been produced by Jenny Tucker of the Sheffield College and Ros Ollin of the School of Education at the University of Huddersfield, which is based in the area covered by Calderdale and Kirklees Training and Enterprise Council of which I am Chief Executive.

We owe them a debt of gratitude for the plain English guide to the assessment process with excellent examples and case studies. I am sure this book will be the standard guide for many years to come.

What we need to remember is that every individual in this country who has responsibility for people at work or young people in schools has to be concerned about competence and how it can be regularly demonstrated as a way of achieving continuous improvement.

This book will convince many that improved performance will be achieved if they build their systems for the development of people around NVQs and GNVQs. By integrating these qualifications around their system of motivating and developing people, they will also improve the quality of supervision and management as assessment and verification become core tasks rather than burdensome additional responsibilities. This integration will also reduce the cost of introducing these qualifications.

Education and training are coming to the centre stage of British life. This book will help us all to strengthen our role in ensuring we achieve full value from the increased investment in time and money that this important development requires.

Alistair Graham
Chairman, Training and Development Lead Body
Chief Executive, Calderdale and Kirklees
Training and Enterprise Council

Preface

The introduction of National and General National Vocational Qualifications (NVQs and GNVQs) with their increased emphasis on quality *assessment* as opposed to quality delivery, has placed assessment practice under the microscope. National standards for training and development have been produced by the Training and Development Lead Body (TDLB), and these standards have been used to create a framework of awards which must be achieved by those involved in the assessment of NVQs and GNVQs. This book aims to provide information and practical advice to anyone wishing to obtain these assessor/verifier/APL (accreditation of prior learning) adviser awards. We hope that it will also provide a basis for questioning the quality of assessment practice in general and give readers a vehicle for examining how competent they really are in the practice of assessment.

This book should be useful in particular to

- candidates working towards becoming an accredited assessor, internal verifier or APL adviser for NVQs and GNVQs
- anyone wishing to gain a deeper understanding of the principles and processes of NVQ and GNVQ assessment, and of current assessment practice
- trainers in assessment practice, who require a reference book for themselves or their candidates
- trainers who wish to compare the original standards with the revised standards.

Please note that this book does *not* include any discussion of the complexities of grading GNVQ assessments.

We feel that the whole question of grading assessment, important and topical as it is, needs to be treated separately, and probably merits a volume to itself. Although we concentrate on the revised National Standards for Assessment and Verification which will be in operation by the end of 1994, we have matched these against the original standards in a grid, and provided guidance for those working to the original standards.

How to use this book

There are four sections, each of which is self-contained, as are the chapters. Each chapter has an introductory guide and summary points, for ease of reference.

Section 1 gives a detailed background to the assessment process and sets it firmly in the context of NVQs and GNVQs. It traces the development of the National Standards for Assessment and Verification and the procedures for quality assurance which have been developed by the National Council for Vocational Qualifications and the awarding bodies. It also deals with the general underpinning knowledge and understanding for assessment required by both candidates and assessors.

Section 2 is a step-by-step guide to the revised standards. It explains the elements and performance criteria and identifies the key points for each performance criterion. At the front of each chapter is a grid matching the original standards against the revised standards currently being introduced. Candidates working to the first issue of the standards will also find specific guidance in this section.

Section 3 is practical guidance on compiling portfolios towards the awards, advice on action planning, evidence collection, and the presentation and assessment of evidence. Throughout the book we have given a range of examples, including samples of completed documentation and case studies based on real-life situations, to help illustrate the points made in the text.

Section 4 includes a comprehensive glossary of assessment-related terminology; *we would urge readers to familiarize themselves with this before turning to the substance of the text* as an understanding of the jargon is vitally important for all concerned. One of the major problems encountered by those coming new to NVQs or GNVQs is getting to grips with the language and terminology involved. This does not just mean understanding what the terms mean, but also feeling an ownership of the language used. Many people involved with these new initiatives are uncomfortable with a language which appears alien, bureaucratic and unrelated to their own work context. Given that a complete revision of the style and language related to assessment seems unlikely, the only solution to this problem is for readers to mentally translate the terms used into language which appears more familiar and appropriate to their own work context.

There are broad and thematic suggestions for further reading in Section 4, rather than references throughout the text, as we consider this to be of more practical use to readers.

Readers should note that the term 'candidate-assessor/verifier/adviser' is used throughout to indicate someone taking an assessor/verifier/APL award; the term 'candidate' refers to those who would be assessed, verified or advised.

Although we have not specifically mentioned Scottish National Vocational Qualifications and General Scottish Vocational Qualifications, this book is equally applicable to those involved assessing these qualifications. We hope readers in Scotland will forgive us, and that they too will find the book of use.

The revised assessment standards (1994) should help to clarify the assessment practice and theory required by assessors. We hope that the background discussion, explanation and examples we have given will assist in improving the quality of the practice of assessment by all those engaged in the important task of the appropriate assessment of National and General National Vocational Qualifications.

Ros Ollin and Jenny Tucker
Sheffield, April 1994

Section 1

Introduction

The intention behind National Vocational Qualifications (NVQs) is to create a coherent national system of qualifications related to specific occupational areas, which can be easily understood, give credit for what people can do as well as what they know, and be achieved independently from any formal programme of learning. This represents a major shift from the traditional model, with assessment often biased towards what people knew in theory rather than their ability to 'do the job' and with qualifications only being achieved after attending a formal course. NVQs have been designed to assess the ability to perform a particular job, without having to take into account the way in which that ability was learned.

Background to NVQs

In the early 1980s, both government and industry recognized the need for improving the skills of the workforce to enable Britain to compete more effectively in overseas markets. To make this improvement possible, a number of factors needed to be addressed. There had to be a systematic identification of what skills were actually needed, an increase in training or retraining where necessary and a straightforward and coherent qualifications framework to provide formal recognition of the skills acquired.

In 1986, the government established the National Council for Vocational Qualifications (NCVQ) to oversee the development of a new qualifications framework based on nationally agreed standards of performance and covering different occupational areas. In order to determine these national standards, Industrial Lead Bodies (ILB) were set up for different occupational areas, eg, construction, hairdressing, containing representatives from employers, industry, related professional bodies and trade unions.

Each lead body was given the responsibility for leading the development of a detailed profile of skills and knowledge required at all levels in the related vocational area. These detailed specifications were based on what an individual has to demonstrate to be considered competent when carrying out work in a particular job role. They also laid down a minimum national standard of performance which had to be met. The Industrial Lead Body then formed these standards into qualifications at different levels, which were packaged and offered by different awarding bodies such as City and Guilds, BTEC, the Electricity Training Association and the Management Verification Consortium. This is still an ongoing process. Some occupational areas do not yet possess an Industry Lead Body and in others where a lead body does exist, qualifications have not yet been produced at all levels.

Key features of NVQs

Traditional vocational qualifications have always been linked to training courses or programmes of study, with students attending either full- or part-time. Although many courses were good, one major criticism was that they concentrated too much on what the programme designers wanted to include, and not enough on what was actually needed at work. National Vocational Qualifications take as their starting point the question, 'What skills and knowledge do particular occupational areas need?' They are then concerned with measuring and accrediting whether someone can actually perform competently within that occupational area. NVQs are:

- based on an analysis of work roles in terms of what functions need to be performed
- led by employers and industry-specific professional bodies – not by 'education'
- focus on *competence* and not whether someone is as good as or better than someone else
- define five different levels of competence
- concentrate on assessment as opposed to delivery.

There are 11 occupational areas covered by NVQs. These are:

- Tending animals, plants and land
- Extracting and providing natural resources
- Constructing
- Engineering
- Manufacturing
- Transporting
- Providing goods and services
- Providing health, social care and protective services
- Providing business services
- Communication and entertaining
- Developing and extending knowledge and skill.

Up-to-date information on all NVQs offered in these areas can be found on the NVQ database provided through NCVQ.

Background to GNVQs

Once NVQs had been established, it became obvious that there was a gap in vocational provision. Whereas NVQs were appropriate for people in employment who would be assessed mainly at their place of work, there was no provision for individuals who were not employed and had not yet made a firm decision about what they wanted to do. This was particularly the case for 16 – 19-year-olds still attending school or college, but who did not wish to go down the 'A' Level route. It was decided that a new, more general qualification was needed that would cover the broad range of skills, knowledge and understanding needed in an occupational area and provide either a route into employment or into further and higher education. As well as accrediting individual achievement within a broad occupational area, it should aim to enhance individual potential and hence, a strong emphasis would be placed on the development of 'core skills' which could be used in any occupation.

Although those in full-time education were the obvious target group, it was also recognized that the qualification could appeal to others not in full-time education, for example, adults not in employment. With these factors in mind, in 1991 the government produced the White Paper *Education and Training for the 21st Century* in which the creation of GNVQs was announced.

Key features of GNVQs

Like NVQs, these are vocationally-oriented qualifications. However, whereas NVQs are related to highly specific job roles and functions, and are designed to be assessed in the workplace, GNVQs relate to far more broadly-based occupational areas and are offered most appropriately in educational establishments such as schools and colleges of further education. The advanced GNVQ (level 3) has been accepted by a number of higher education establishments as an entry qualification and it is possible that GNVQ level 4 may be offered in higher education sometime in the future. Because of the needs of higher education to have some point of comparison between applicants, it was decided to offer grades of pass, merit and distinction within the qualification. These grades are determined at the end of the programme, and are based on a selected third of all the work presented by an individual.

NVQ and GNVQs
Based on units which are credited separately
Units can be accumulated for a full qualification
Units contain elements, p.c.* and range
Time taken/methods to achieve – irrelevant
Based on outcomes not input
Judged on evidence produced by candidate
Open access to assessment
Possibility of credit for prior learning

*performance criteria

Figure 1.1 *Similarities between NVQs and GNVQs*

NVQs	GNVQs
Occupational competence	Broad-based vocational education
Assessment of competence in workplace	Assessment of achievement
Standards devised by industry lead bodies	Standards devised by NCVQ and awarding bodies
No grading – only competent or not yet competent	Grading portfolio at end – pass/merit/ distinction

Figure 1.2 *Differences between NVQs and GNVQs*

By 1996, there will be 14 occupational areas covered by GNVQs. These are:

- Leisure and tourism
- Manufacturing
- Art and design
- Business
- Health and social care
- Science
- Hospitality and catering
- Construction and built environment
- Management
- Distribution
- Information technology
- Engineering
- Agriculture
- Media/performing arts.

Every GNVQ is made up of a set number of vocational units, some of which are mandatory and others which can be selected from a number of options, and core skill units in communications, information technology, and application of numbers. There are other optional core skill units in working with others, improving own learning and performance, and problem solving.

Assessment of NVQs and GNVQs

There are a number of significant differences between NVQs and GNVQs. NVQs are intended to be firmly based in the work context and designed for accrediting the skills of working people and providing a system for identifying where skills need to be acquired or updated. There is no programme of learning built into the qualification. GNVQs are usually for the younger age group and their context is far more educational with the probability that some delivery of learning will be involved. Students will learn through student-centred programmes which emphasize the development of personal skills –

core skills – as well as occupational skills. However, in spite of the differences in target group and style of provision, there are significant similarities in assessment practice. It is these similarities which interest us here.

Both NVQs and GNVQs are based on the same principles of assessment. They are both assessed to national standards, on the basis of evidence presented by the candidate, and are committed to promoting equality of access to assessment regardless of disability, geographical location, religion, ethnic group or gender. Hence the assessment process and the considerations to be taken into account are very similar in spite of the 'cultural' differences of work and education. It is because of the similarities in the assessment process, together with the intention to maximize transferability within the qualifications framework, that NCVQ wishes to ensure consistency in assessment methods and practices. This is why all assessors, APL advisers and internal verifiers for both NVQs and GNVQs need to achieve the appropriate accredited award, ie, D32, D33, D34, D35 or D36.

1981   **New Training Initiative** *(Manpower Service Commission [MSC])*
Identified need to increase skills of workforce to cope with new patterns of working, developments in new technology and increased competition from overseas. First mention of need for 'Standards of a new kind'.

1986   **Review of Vocational Qualifications: A Report by the Working Group** *(MSC and Department of Education and Science)*
Concluded that there was a low take-up of vocational qualifications. Perceived by employers as relying too much on theory as opposed to practice. Confusion and overlap on the provision available, with difficulties in access, progression and transfer of credits. Problems with methods of assessment and little recognition of learning outside formal programmes.

1986   **Education and Training – Working Together** *(Government White Paper)*
Proposed the development of new qualifications based on national standards defined by industry and operating within a coherent qualifications structure.

1986   **National Council of Vocational Qualification (NCVQ) established**
To carry out proposals from the White Paper including the accreditation of standards, development of new qualifications framework, development of NVQs, liaison with awarding bodies and monitoring of quality assurance procedures. NCVQ was set up as an independent body with intital government funding covering England, Wales and Northern Ireland. It has no legal powers but must promote the new vocational initiative through cooperation with relevant bodies. The Scottish Council for Vocational Education and Training (SCOTVEC) has the same remit in Scotland.

1986   **New Occupational Standards Branch created at MSC**
Given responsibility for setting up industry lead bodies to develop occupational standards. Where possible, the lead bodies built on existing organizations, eg Industrial Training Boards such as the Construction Industry Training Board (CITB).

1988   **Employment for the 1990s** *(Government White Paper)*
Reaffirmed the need for standards and qualifications based on competence and recognized by employers. Proposed establishment of local Training and Enterprise Councils (TECs) to be responsible at local level for the planning and delivery of vocational training and enterprise programmes.

1990	Training Agency (formerly MSC) becomes absorbed in the Training, Enterprise and Education Directorate (TEED) at the Department of Employment

1991 Education and Training for the 21st Century *(Government White Paper)*
Proposed that General National Vocational Qualifications – designed to provide broad-based vocational preparation – should be introduced into the national qualifications framework:

1992 National Targets for Education and Training announced
These set targets for young people, adults and employers;

Foundation Learning:
• by 1997, 80 per cent of young people to reach NVQ level 2 or equivalent
• all young people who can benefit to receive training and education to NVQ level 3 or equivalent
• by 2000, 50 per cent of young people to reach NVQ level 3 or equivalent

Lifelong Learning:
• by 1996, all employees to be given training and development
• by 1996, 50 per cent of workforce to be working towards NVQs
• by 2000, 50 per cent of workforce to be qualified to NVQ level 3 or equivalent.

1993 GNVQ Levels given names instead of numbers
Level 3 'Advanced' (also to be known as the 'Vocational "A" Level')
Level 2 'Intermediate'
Level 1 'Foundation'

1994 Competitiveness: Helping Businesses to Win (Government White Paper)
£300m to be spent on strengthening education and training

Figure 1.3 *Background to NVQs and GNVQs*

I NVQs/GNVQs and the Assessment Process

The Training and Development Lead Body standards; assessment as part of the training cycle; the assessment process.

Assessment as part of the training cycle

The Training and Development Lead Body standards

Both NVQs and GNVQs focus on the assessment of what someone can actually do rather than how they acquired that skill or knowledge. However, as the assessor and verifier awards are made up of elements from the Training and Development Lead Body standards which reflect the *whole* training cycle, this chapter will look briefly at how these awards fit into the overall framework. It will then concentrate on the five stages involved in the assessment process.

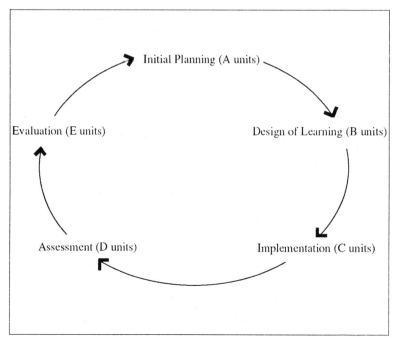

Figure 1.1 *The TDLB Training Cycle*

How the 'D' units got their name

There are a number of different models for the training process, but although the terms may vary from one model to another, the essential stages are similar in nature. They all have the following features:

- *Initial planning* – usually takes the form of an initial diagnosis of what the candidate already knows and what they need to learn
- *Design of learning* – decisions are made and agreements are reached on what the outcomes of learning should be, how the learning is to take place, what methods and resources will be used and what timescale is appropriate
- *Implementation* – the learning programme is put into practice
- Assessment – the results of learning are assessed
- *Evaluation* – the overall effectiveness of the process is evaluated.

The TDLB standards follow the training cycle and contain five classifications from A to E:

A. All elements beginning with A refer to the *planning* stage
B. All elements beginning with B refer to the *design of learning* stage
C. All elements beginning with C refer to the *implementation* stage
D. All elements beginning with D refer to the *assessment* stage
E. All elements beginning with E refer to the *evaluation* stage.

To produce the assessor and verifier awards, elements were taken from the TDLB standards related to assessment and formed into units (hence the 'D' units). These will be explained in greater detail in Chapter 2 and in the step-by-step guides, but depending on your job role you will need one or more of the following:

D32 – for assessment of performance (eg, someone carrying out a task or procedure)
D33 – for assessment using diverse evidence (ie, a variety of different types of evidence)
D34 – for verifying the assessment procedures within an organization (internal verifier)
D36 – for giving advice on Accreditation of Prior Learning (APL adviser).

There are two other 'D' units we have not specifically covered in this book. These are units D35 for external verification of the assessment process and D31 on designing assessment systems. However, much of the information given in the following pages will be relevant to these awards.

The NVQ/GNVQ assessment process

Most people involved in assessment will be covering the assessment process as a natural part of their work, and the five stages involved will be familiar to them, although they may not have identified these stages explicitly. This process is particularly reflected in the units D32 and D33 which require evidence that all these stages of assessment are adequately covered. In this section we will be looking in detail at what each stage actually involves.

Stage 1	Stage 2	Stage 3	Stage 4	Stage 5
Planning for Assessment	Collecting Evidence	Making Judgements	Giving Feedback	Recording Achievement

Figure 1.2 *Stages of the assessment process*

Stage 1: Planning for assessment

In order to make sure that assessment is absolutely fair, no candidate should ever have a 'surprise' assessment. He or she should always have been involved in the planning stage and will have agreed to the assessment taking place. Obviously, the level of involvement may vary according to the ability of the candidate and the context in which the planning takes place. A candidate with learning difficulties working towards an NVQ level 1 will almost certainly need a lot of help and guidance. However, they can still be given opportunities to make their own suggestions and choices without putting them in a situation where they feel overwhelmed.

The assessor and the candidate will usually meet to plan how and when particular elements or units are going to be assessed. If the assessor is working in the same place as the candidate, then the meetings should be easy to arrange and, once the candidate understands the assessment process, quite short. For a tutor or a trainer assessing candidates for NVQs or GNVQs in an educational or training setting, it is likely that they will be meeting on a frequent basis, possibly with regular tutorial times arranged. For the assessor who is not in regular contact with the candidate, arranging a planning meeting by telephone or letter is vital.

Although planning for assessment will often take place on an individual basis, there may be times, particularly in schools or colleges, where the planning takes place with a whole group of candidates. This might be because a specific activity, eg, an assignment, has been set up which covers a number of competences. Whatever way the planning meeting takes place, both candidate(s) and assessor need to be clear on a number of key areas:

- *What* competences will be assessed?
- *When* will they be assessed?
- *Where* will they be assessed?
- *How* will they be assessed?

Examples of planning for assessment

- A candidate working towards an NVQ in motor vehicle repair is assessed at the garage where he works. As the assessor in this case is the owner of the garage, and they see each other every day, arrangements for assessment take place on a fairly continuous basis. They also take advantage of spontaneous opportunities for assessment, eg, the candidate suddenly gets a job which will give him the chance to demonstrate a particular competence and so arranges, more or less on the spot, that he should be observed and assessed. The key to this type of planning is that both need to spend time initially getting familiar with the competences required for the NVQ and with how assessments should be organized. They also need to establish a procedure for taking advantage of these 'spontaneous' opportunities that may occur.

- A candidate working towards an NVQ in beauty therapy is being assessed by an outside assessor. They have a planning meeting where they discuss what competences still need to be demonstrated and decide that competences related to nail care have not yet been covered. The candidate gives the assessor a number of dates and times when she will be carrying out a full nail treatment and they arrange a convenient time for the assessor to come and observe her. They then check if any other competences could be covered at the same time and decide that the candidate could also be assessed on some elements related to health and safety and customer care.

- Catering students at a local college working in a training restaurant have a group meeting with their tutor before they go into a lunch-time session where they are serving at table. They agree on a number of competences that they should have the opportunity to demonstrate during that time and which can be observed and assessed.

- A candidate wishing to submit evidence for APL towards an NVQ in furniture upholstery has a preliminary meeting with her APL adviser. During this meeting the adviser helps the candidate to match her past experience against the requirements of the NVQ and works with her to identify what evidence will be appropriate to support her claim and how to prepare her portfolio of evidence. They agree on an appropriate timescale and possible date for assessment. During this planning meeting the adviser explains his role, making a clear differentiation between the adviser role and the entirely separate role of assessor. He then tells the candidate who the assessor is likely to be and agrees to make arrangements for assessment after their next meeting.

- Students who are candidates on a GNVQ programme are given an assignment by a tutor during a classroom session. The briefing for this assignment gives instructions on what needs to be presented for assessment, when it should be presented and the criteria against which it will be assessed.

In all of these cases, the planning process should be accompanied by the appropriate documentation recording the details of what will be assessed and any action that needs to be taken prior to assessment. This documentation is called the assessment plan. Assessment plans are covered in more detail in Chapters 9 and 10.

Stage 2: Collecting the evidence

'Evidence' is usually associated with a legal situation where information, documents or witness testimony are produced to prove the defendant innocent or guilty. It would be wrong to suggest candidates for NVQs are guilty of incompetence until they provide the evidence to prove themselves innocent; they have not *yet* demonstrated competence. However, it is useful to bear in mind the rigorous examination given to legal evidence to assess its worth. For example, a legal witness has to be credible and consistent in their testimony and able to stand up to cross-examination. Legal documents always need the signatures of reputable persons to confirm that they are truthful and accurate. Circumstantial evidence, along the lines of, 'Well, he was there at the time, so he must have done it!' is not sufficient, and there must be other hard evidence to back it up.

Just as in a court of law, the evidence produced for an NVQ or GNVQ should be of good quality and be able to stand up to rigorous examination. Hence the candidate should be clear, not only about what they have to do or produce which will provide evidence, but also what *quality* of evidence is needed. During the planning for assessment they should have been able to discuss:

- what evidence is appropriate to meet the specified performance criteria
- what knowledge might be assessed
- arrangements for the assessment
- how the evidence will be assessed.

Candidates should also have discussed the best way to go about collecting evidence. In many cases they will have been helped to produce an action plan which identifies what they need to do. Examples of action plans can be found in Chapter 9. Evidence may be collected in three different ways:

- *Performance evidence*: by being observed carrying out a task or procedure which occurs naturally in a work situation, by producing relevant items they have made or repaired, by doing a project, assignment or simulation which has been especially set up for assessment purposes.
- *Differing sources of evidence*: by presenting a variety of different types of evidence (eg, natural performance, memos they have written, witness testimonies, completed assignments, photographs of them involved in a relevant activity, etc.).
- *Evidence from prior experience*: by using relevant evidence from past activities and situations in which candidates have been involved.

Evidence can be:

■ *Direct* – it reflects their own work, ie, the candidate either performs it or produces it themselves.

■ *Indirect* – other people or other sources provide the information about the candidate's work, ie, a third party confirms that the candidate is competent in a particular area. This 'third party' can be a person such as an employer or a customer who produces a statement about the candidate, or it can be a qualification which the candidate has achieved.

Stage 3: Making judgements

Once the evidence is presented, the assessor needs to judge whether it proves that the candidate has met the required elements and performance criteria. When making these judgements, the assessor needs to take a number of different things into account. The terms used in Figure 1.3 are the most common – and the most important – terms involved in assessment judgements. All these conditions need to be met by the evidence provided. Let us look more closely at each of these in turn.

Validity
■ *The assessment process and the evidence required should be appropriate to what is being assessed.*

It would not be valid to assess whether a cook could bake a cake by asking them to draw a picture of one. Nor would it be valid to assess whether a gardener could plant bulbs by watching them sow seeds. Valid assessment implies that the method (or methods) used are the ones most likely to give an accurate picture of that individual's competence within a particular area.

Old-fashioned methods of assessing a student's ability in a foreign language often lacked validity. It is amazing to think that a person's ability to communicate in French was tested by completing a series of written grammatical exercises rather than on whether they could actually speak and be understood!

COMPETENT		NOT COMPETENT
	EVIDENCE	
Valid	◄ ············· ►	Not Valid
Reliable	◄ ············· ►	Not Reliable
Sufficient	◄ ············· ►	Not Sufficient
Authentic	◄ ············· ►	Not Authentic
Current	◄ ············· ►	Not Current

Figure 1.3 *Terms used in assessment judgements*

Validity has a particular significance in NVQs because what is being assessed is the evidence presented. If the evidence is not valid, ie, it is not an appropriate means of demonstrating competence, then the candidate will have to be reassessed using different, or additional and more relevant evidence. What is important to grasp is that no evidence is automatically valid or not valid. It is the candidate's interpretation of that evidence and how they justify its relevance that makes it valid.

For example, a photograph of the candidate and another person could be presented as evidence. By itself that photograph has no meaning. However, if the candidate says 'This is a photograph which appeared in my firm's newsheet showing me receiving a prize for apprentice of the year', the photograph takes on a meaning and becomes valid evidence (as long as the candidate can prove that it is true). This is why explanatory statements related to any documentary evidence presented are important, as they can give the reasons why the candidate believes a particular piece of evidence to be valid.

Reliability
- *The judgement confirms that the candidate's performance will be of a consistent standard in a range of different contexts.*
- *The same judgement would be made about the candidate by the same assessor on a number of different occasions.*
- *The same judgement would be made about the candidate by other assessors.*

Reliability and fairness are closely linked. The candidate must have confidence that they will be treated fairly by assessors, that they are not going to have a harsher assessment from one assessor than from another, or that another candidate is going to be assessed more leniently than themselves. They also need to be sure that they will not be discriminated against because of some personal prejudice of the assessor. Most of us would probably agree that many of us interpret guidelines differently, or consider some aspects of work more important than others. These can all affect our judgements and make them different from candidate to candidate, and different from someone else doing the same assessment; hence measures which ensure consistency are essential if we are to be fair to the candidate. Consistency in NVQs and GNVQs is also essential for employers or educational institutions, who will be asked to accept that the standards give a clear and accurate picture of how someone can perform in employment or in preparation for a higher education programme. These bodies will need to rely on the quality and consistency of the judgements being made.

Sufficiency
- *The evidence is enough to prove competence.*

Although the disease of evidence overload is being experienced by assessors who are presented with large numbers of lever-arch files containing evidence from just one candidate, there is a fine line between adding evidence for the sake of it and ensuring that the evidence is sufficient to prove competence. Often candidates provide far too much evidence. In our experience, *insufficient evidence* does not usually mean too little evidence but *too little evidence of a relevant kind*. This can result from a 'shopping trolley' approach to the assessment where all sorts of items are dropped in in the vague hope that they will provide something of substance. If being assessed is to have some meaning for the candidate, then the thought required in discussing their own performance, in assessing their own strengths and areas for development and in working out which evidence is most appropriate to demonstrate which competence, is an essential part of the process. Without this disciplined identification and selection the candidate will remain unaware of what it is that they do or know that enables them to perform a particular work role. Here are some examples of insufficient evidence:

- letter from employer which is too vague and does not refer to specific competences (see chapter 10 for example of good practice here)
- document included without any explanation as to why it is valid
- only one observation of someone performing a task
- GNVQ assignment – answered in too little detail, and not to the standard required.

Authenticity
- *The evidence is genuine and has been produced by the candidate.*

With some assessment methods, such as end-of-term examinations, traditional safeguards have been established to ensure that candidates cannot cheat. An independent invigilator watches them while they write their answers, there are rules about what items of equipment can be present and strict rules of secrecy about what they might be required to answer.

In both NVQs and GNVQs, these types of safeguards may also be possible. Candidates on GNVQs are still required to achieve a minimum score of 70 per cent in externally set unit end-tests before they can gain the qualification. NVQs may have some knowledge requirements which can, under certain circumstances, be assessed by a written test. In these cases, the assessor will naturally apply the appropriate safeguards against copying or cheating.

Determining whether performance evidence is genuine will obviously be reasonably straightforward if the assessor is observing the candidate actually doing something at work. However, the assessor has to be sure that any end product presented by the candidate as 'one I made earlier' really has been produced by them. Assessors might also have to decide whether evidence presented from prior experience is authentic or produced through some 'imaginative' forgery, with co-opted friends and relatives providing the necessary signatures!

Just as with all other evidence, it is important that the judgements made are fair and reliable. One instance where this might be particularly problematic is in the assessment of individual contributions to group work which may occur in GNVQ assessments. The assessor needs to use every means at his or her disposal both to ensure that they give fair recognition to every contribution, but also that they do not give the non-contributors the 'benefit of the doubt' and give them the same positive assessment as the rest.

Currency
■   *The evidence can prove that the candidate is up to date on current methods and equipment required in the appropriate occupational area.*

Some examples of where this issue could occur:

■   A candidate for NVQ in business administration worked in an office 15 years ago. Would this provide evidence that they could work in an office now?
■   A candidate for NVQ in training and development has a teaching qualification obtained in 1976. Would this provide evidence that they could work in a training environment now?
■   A candidate for an NVQ in aircraft maintenance engineering has been off work for two years because of an accident. Would they still be up to date with the skills and technology required?

There are no hard and fast rules here. Obviously every occupational area is different and some change far more quickly than others. However, as a general rule, areas which deal primarily with people can use evidence which dates back over a greater number of years than occupational areas where rapid changes in technology are likely to make skills obsolete – even those acquired only a few years before.

Stage 4: Giving feedback

NVQs have been accused of being a mechanical system of ticking boxes and recording results and, like any system, they can be treated in a minimalist fashion. GNVQs, because they take place in an educational context, have not met with quite the same level of criticism. However, if the stages of the assessment process are covered sensitively and with integrity, both qualifications can provide a developmental experience for candidates. One stage which is fundamental in any development process is the feedback stage, where the candidate is given specific information about what they have achieved or not achieved. The candidate is also given the opportunity to discuss this fully with the assessor. An important word in this context is 'discuss', implying a two-way process of identifying strengths and areas for improvement with the assessor using a considerable amount of skill in involving the candidate in analysing what, if anything, needs to be improved before the next assessment. The step-by-step guides and the feedback section in Chapter 3 will give more details about the process of constructive feedback.

Stage 5: Recording achievement

The final stage in the assessment process is to record the results so that:

- there is clear documentation on what the candidate has already achieved
- there is a clear record of what else needs to be assessed if they are to achieve a qualification
- there is a written record that can be accessed by other assessors and verifiers.

Summary

This chapter should have helped you with the following:

- how the 'D' units got their name
- key stages in the assessment process
- key terms in the assessment process.

2 Key Roles in the NVQ/GNVQ Assessment Process

Assessment systems; the role of the candidate; the role of the adviser; the role of the first-line assessor; the role of the second-line assessor; the role of the internal verifier; the role of the external verifier.

Quality assurance is a vital part of any national qualifications system. All national assessment systems need to ensure that everyone involved in the assessment of candidates is assessing correctly, working to agreed procedures and to an agreed standard of performance. This cannot just be left on trust to individual assessors but needs to be part of a strict monitoring framework which covers not only the individual assessor, but all the assessment within an organization and, finally, all the assessment nationally.

However, any system is only as good as the people who take part in it and the quality of skills and knowledge of those involved are key factors in making the system credible and worthwhile. This chapter will be looking at the NVQ/GNVQ assessment system, the roles people play in it and the essential skills and knowledge they need.

Assessment systems

Most assessment systems, including those for traditional qualifications, have

WHO?	Candidate/Assessor/Verifier
WHAT?	Skills/Knowledge/Understanding to be assessed
WHEN?	Appropriate place(s), time(s) and opportunity(ies) for assessment
HOW?	• Criteria for achievement/non-achievement (in some systems pass/fail) • Procedures for informing the candidate of requirements • Procedures for assessment • Procedures for informing candidate of results of assessment • Procedures for documenting the results of assessment • Procedures for monitoring the assessment is accurate

Figure 2.1 *Components of an assessment system*

a number of aspects in common. They involve people who play key roles within the process of assessment, they specify what areas of knowledge and skill are to be assessed, they identify the circumstances in which assessment should take place, they lay down the parameters for achievement or non-achievement and identify procedures for carrying out and documenting the assessment.

Key roles

Within the NVQ assessment system there are a number of key roles. These include:

- the person designing the methods for assessment
- the candidate being assessed
- the adviser or counsellor who helps the candidate prepare for assessment
- the assessor who assesses the candidate's performance
- the assessor who assesses the candidate's competence using evidence from a variety of sources
- the internal verifier who ensures that the first two assessment roles are being carried out correctly within the organization
- the external verifier who monitors the assessment procedures on a regional or national level.

The assessment design role (D31)

This is the individual or team that identifies clearly what needs to be assessed, determines the most appropriate methods to use in assessment and then designs, for example, relevant tests or assignments. They are also concerned with developing useful systems for carrying out assessments, such as creating checklists which can help in observation, or working out a set of procedures for assessing core skills as an integrated part of a GNVQ programme. They are also concerned with ensuring that all materials and methods used follow good equal opportunities practice.

The candidate role

In traditional programmes, the candidate has often been someone that assessment is 'done to' without their previous experience being taken into account and without the opportunity for them to be involved in the process. So, in the past, an examination question for telephone engineers on a day-release course might have been along the lines of 'Write an essay of between 600 and 800 words on the history of the telephone'. In a situation such as this, the 'evidence' required of the candidate was not dependent on who they were or what they had done; everyone, irrespective of background or experience, had to answer the same questions. Nor was the evidence the most valid means of showing that they were capable of doing the job of telephone engineer.

During the last 20 years, much has been done by some awarding bodies to introduce methods of assessment that are more closely related to real-life work requirements and to place more responsibility with the student to assess their own performance. The NVQ/GNVQ assessment system builds on some of these earlier developments. Although NVQs and GNVQs obviously prescribe what skills or knowledge need to be demonstrated, the position of the candidate is changed into one of *active* involvement in their own assessment, placing the responsibility for identifying and collecting the evidence for assessment with the candidate. Obviously, the candidate may need advice and sometimes a substantial amount of guidance and support from the adviser or assessor. However, it is important to remember that a candidate who is familiar with the procedures and evidence required could, in theory, collect and present evidence for assessment without any input or advice from another source.

The adviser/counsellor role (D36)

This can be both a formal and an informal role. In its formal sense the role is most commonly undertaken as 'APL (or APEL (accreditation of prior experience and learning) or APA (accreditation of prior achievement) adviser', although at least one awarding body uses the term 'counsellor' instead of 'adviser'. The main responsibilities of the adviser begin with an initial guidance interview where the process of APL is explained and the candidate is encouraged to reflect on their previous learning and experience. From this, the candidate is helped to establish whether any of this might provide evidence which could be accredited towards units or qualifications in particular occupational areas. The candidate is then helped to select the occupational area of most interest and relevance and to identify more specifically what evidence would be appropriate and the best way of generating it. An action plan is agreed between the adviser and the candidate which identifies specific evidence, action to be taken to collect it and the timescale involved. The adviser remains in contact to offer advice about the quality of the evidence and to help the candidate decide on an appropriate time for formal assessment. Finally, the adviser will make arrangements with an accredited assessor to assess the candidate against the units or elements claimed.

The formal advisory role, not just for APL but for NVQs and GNVQs in general, can often occur in a group induction or training session for prospective candidates where general information and guidance are given on compiling a portfolio of evidence. The adviser then follows this up with individual guidance interviews.

The assessor role

Direct Assessment of Performance (D32) (first-line assessor, front-line assessor, workplace assessor)
The most straightforward way of finding out if someone is competent in a

Someone using a piece of equipment:	a forester using a chainsaw
	a hairdresser using a hair dryer
Someone performing a service:	a care assistant giving a bed bath
	a waiter/ress serving a drink
Someone carrying out procedures:	a kitchen assistant following rules of hygiene
	a gas service engineer observing safety procedures
Someone showing a particular skill:	a student working well in a group
	a manager establishing and maintaining trust with his or her subordinates
Someone making a product:	a joiner making a cupboard
	a bricklayer building a wall
	a student producing an assignment

Figure 2.2 *Examples of performance evidence*

particular area of work is to actually watch them doing it. A hairdresser might write essays about hair styling, produce testimonials from satisfied clients and previous employers and display photographs of hairstyles he or she has created. These would all be valuable evidence, but the surest and most natural way of establishing whether someone can do the job is for an assessor to observe him or her in a hairdressing salon, styling and cutting people's hair – in other words, in watching the candidate 'perform'. The other way an assessor might assess directly is by looking at something the candidate has produced, eg, a cupboard made by a joiner; an assignment produced by a student.

The assessor who carries out this function is given different titles by different awarding bodies. We shall be using the term 'first line assessor' throughout this book. The assessor in this 'first line' role will probably be one of the following:

- a supervisor or manager in the workplace
- a trainer in a workshop
- a tutor at a school, college or university.

Assessment using evidence from differing sources (diverse evidence)
(D33) (second-line assessor)
The 'second-line' assessor draws on a variety of different sources of

evidence, not only performance evidence, to make their assessment decision. These sources could include among others:

- other evidence from the candidate, such as a log book or diary
- a report from the candidate or from the candidate's peers
- judgements from other assessors
- evidence from the candidate's prior experience.

The need for this other evidence is based on the idea that competence often entails more complex skills, particularly at the higher levels.

The majority of jobs involve a range of situations which need different skills and abilities. In more complex jobs many different competences are required, not all of which can be assessed through direct observation of performance. Take, for example, a situation where a manager in a local government office is working towards an NVQ in management. Although this manager could be observed for a limited period of time, it would be grossly expensive and time-consuming to observe them to make sure that they could perform *all* the aspects of the manager's role. Even then it is unlikely that all aspects of that role would actually be covered. However, the second-line assessor could use other sources of evidence to ensure that this manager was competent including testimonies from line managers and colleagues, examples of written communications such as memos and letters, or minutes of meetings chaired by the candidate. The collation and judgement of this variety of sources of evidence will give a more rounded picture of the candidate's knowledge, ability and skills. In a GNVQ, the 'second-line' assessor would be making assessments which cover a broad-based set of occupational skills and knowledge and would probably be working with other assessors within the programme team. The 'second-line' assessor needs to be able to assess all these different sources of evidence with the same kind of rigour as assessing performance. The assessor in this 'second-line' role would be:

either – a member of the assessment staff working with first-line assessors

or – the *same* person as the first-line assessor,

ie, the two roles would be combined so that they could assess both performance and diverse evidence.

The internal verifier role

Internally verify the assessment process (D34)
This role is a very important one in the quality assurance of NVQs and GNVQs. Within all but the smallest organizations, there will probably be more than one person acting in the assessor role. There may be a variety of occupational areas being covered, there may be a number of assessors who are working in the same occupational area and assessing the same

competences but with different candidates, and there may be assessors who are assessing *different* competences but with the *same* candidates. In all these situations, what is vital is that the assessments are consistent and reliable and conform to national standards of assessment. It is the internal verifier's role to see that this happens by ensuring that:

- all staff have had the necessary training including obtaining the necessary assessor awards
- assessors are given all the necessary help and information they need to be able to assess effectively
- the quality of assessments is monitored on a regular basis
- they are available to answer queries if assessors experience difficulties.

In a larger organization, there may be a number of people acting in the role of internal verifier. They will obviously have to communicate with each other to make sure that information and procedures are fully consistent. Internal verifiers provide the main link between the assessors in their organization and the external verifier.

The external verifier role (D35)

As NVQs are a national system, there is obviously a need for monitoring of quality and consistency at a national level. This is done through a network of external verifiers appointed through specific awarding bodies whose role is to visit different centres offering NVQs or GNVQs and monitor that assessment and internal verification procedures are being carried out correctly. As the external verifier is the main link with the awarding body, she or he should also be the person who can give the definitive answer to queries from centres, eg, on the acceptability of certain evidence or on the interpretation of certain performance criteria.

National Council for Vocational Qualifications

The final link in the quality assurance chain is NCVQ itself. All awarding bodies have to apply for accreditation and then submit themselves for re-accreditation on a regular basis. If NCVQ are not satisfied with the quality of the assessment and verification procedures, accreditation to award NVQs or GNVQs will be withdrawn.

Different combinations of roles

Within the roles identified there are obviously opportunities for different combinations and variations depending on the nature and size of the organization. For example, there is frequently an *informal* advisory role with any candidate, helping them to identify and produce evidence, whether of prior learning and experience or of current achievement. This advisory role is often adopted by the individual who will later formally assess the candidate. However, one combination of roles that should never occur is that of assessor and

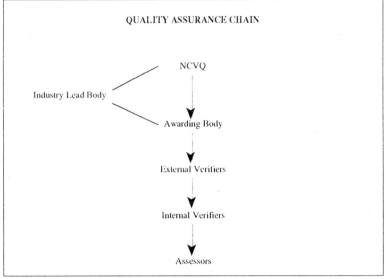

Figure 2.3 *NVQ/GNVQ Quality Assurance Chain*

internal verifier with the *same* candidate. Obviously, that does not prevent someone from acting as an assessor with one candidate and then as an internal verifier with a candidate that someone else has assessed.

Case Study 1
A candidate working in a large engineering firm is assessed on her use of a particular piece of equipment by being observed and then questioned by her immediate supervisor, acting in the role of 'first-line' assessor. The supervisor from another section acts as the 'second-line' assessor, assessing her on the other evidence provided in addition to the 'performance' evidence – in this case a letter of validation from her previous employer and a certificate showing an engineering qualification she obtained three years before. The senior manager of the section acts as the internal verifier monitoring the process and procedures of the assessment.

Case Study 2
A candidate who is a student on a GNVQ in health and social care programme put on by his local college is given an assignment by his tutor on care provision for the elderly. Before the assignment, he has been given an individual interview with his tutor who has acted in the informal role of adviser, giving him help on how to approach the assignment. The same tutor will act as a 'first-line' assessor observing the candidate work with the elderly in a day-care centre and assessing the assignment produced as a result. The same tutor will also act as a 'second-line' assessor, assessing the candidate's work diary and using the feedback given by the supervisor and other

staff working in the home for the elderly to make a final assessment judgement. The programme coordinator will take on the role of the internal verifier.

Case Study 3
A candidate with considerable management experience, working within a local authority, wishes to claim APL towards an NVQ in management for what she has achieved in the past. One of the local authority training officers, acting in the adviser's role, discusses with her what evidence would be appropriate. Another training officer acts in the assessor's role and makes an assessment judgement on the evidence. The line manager from another section who has achieved D34 acts as internal verifier.

Summary

This chapter should have helped you with the following:

- the NVQ and GNVQ assessment system
- key roles in the assessment system
- how these roles fit in with different work environments.

3 Knowledge and Skills to Perform the Roles

Assessment types; fair and reliable assessment; assessment methods – observation, oral and written questioning, skills with people, skills in feedback.

All the roles mentioned in Chapter 2 need a high level of skill in order to carry them out effectively. These skills are not purely mechanical: they involve the ability to analyse, to choose appropriately, to transfer across different contexts, to be sensitive to individual needs and to absorb and communicate substantial amounts of information. The ability to carry out such activities can only occur in conjunction with the knowledge and understanding of different methods and practices involved in assessment, of different strategies for working with people and of some awareness of the ethical context in which anyone in a potentially powerful role should operate. This chapter gives some details of different types and methods of assessment and then considers some of the more 'people-based' skills that are needed to perform these roles.

Types of assessment

Criterion-referenced

Both NVQs and GNVQs are criterion-referenced systems of assessment, ie, the candidate is assessed against a set of pre-established criteria. These criteria represent a consensus of opinion over what forms the basis of an 'acceptable' standard. In a sense, all occupational areas are already based on criterion-referenced systems. For example, if a car was having its brakes mended, the owner would want to feel confident that the mechanic was working to an acceptable set of standards within the motor industry. Similarly, a patient being looked after by a nurse would want to feel that he or she was performing her duties to the same standard as a nurse in any other hospital in the country. The creation of sets of national standards for different occupational areas is a reflection of what has traditionally occurred in practice, although there is, of course, some controversy over whether the criteria identified in the standards are always the right ones.

In assessments made against criteria, there are only two possible outcomes for a candidate. They can either be judged competent against the criteria or not yet competent against the criteria. For example, in vehicle body repair, a candidate fitting replacement body panels either *does* position the replacement components according to the vehicle manufacturer's specifications, in which case he or she is competent against that criterion, or *does not*, in which case he or she is not yet competent against that criterion. However, there are obviously many situations where the judgement of competence is more problematic, particularly where the language appears to allow for subjective judgement and we will be covering these later in the chapter.

Norm-referenced

Traditional academic programmes are based on norm-referenced systems where the achievement of the candidate is judged in comparison to the achievement of other candidates. Hence in programmes such as 'A' levels and GCSEs, candidates who get an 'A' grade are judged to be better than candidates who have obtained a 'C' grade and, as norm-referenced systems, have their basis in the idea that a few will do well, most will do averagely and some will do poorly. That means there is an expectation that a few people will get 'A' grades, a large number of people will get 'C' grades and some will get 'E' or even 'F' grades. If one year it turns out that a large number of people obtain 'A' grades, the system would be studied closely and revised – either the examinations would be made more difficult, or the examiners making the assessments would be told to assess more strictly. Hence there is no real notion of 'fixed' standards.

To clarify a major problem in the norm-referenced system, let us consider our previous example of the patient being looked after by the nurse. It would be no consolation to the patient that the nurse was the best in the country, if the general standards of nursing care nationally were inadequate and the nurse was merely the best out of a very poorly skilled profession. The problem, then, with norm-referencing is that comparisons only suggest that someone is better or worse, they do not suggest what the minimum standard for performance or achievement actually is. However, it is true that many employers and higher education establishments do place an emphasis on the

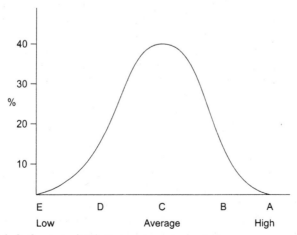

Figure 3.1 *Performance distribution curve*

achievement of high grades and that norm-referencing does provide a means of distinguishing between individual employees or students.

GNVQs are attempting to combine the best of both worlds by making their units *criterion-referenced* so that minimum acceptable standards are clearly identified, but *norm-referencing* by awarding a pass, merit or distinction, based on the work completed overall, hence enabling comparison with the achievements of other GNVQ candidates nationally.

Formative

Every time a candidate receives a judgement on their performance which will cause them to alter certain aspects of it, they are receiving formative assessment, ie, assessment which 'forms' their development towards a certain desired goal, just as a metal worker 'forms' a hot piece of metal towards a certain desired shape. This type of assessment takes place on a continuous basis sometimes formally, but very often informally. Formative assessment which is carried out helpfully and sympathetically can play a large part in motivating candidates, particularly those unsure of their own abilities.

Case studies in formative assessment

1. A candidate working in a restaurant is constantly receiving feedback on his performance by the head waiter. From the simple reminder, 'You've forgotten the table napkins' to a full debriefing on how he served at table on a busy Saturday night, the head waiter is providing feedback that will shape the candidate's future performance to the desired goal of being the perfect waiter. If the candidate is working towards an NVQ this formative assessment will also give him an indication of when he will be ready for a formal end assessment.

2. A candidate working towards an NVQ in training and development is receiving formative assessments from a number of different people. From her supervisor, who sits in on some of her training sessions, from other trainers in her area of work with whom she discusses various aspects of her work on a regular basis and from the people she is training, who she asks to evaluate each session she leads. These are in addition to the more formal formative assessment that she has received from her official assessor who has made a diagnostic observation visit to one of the candidate's sessions.

3. A candidate for GNVQ science has regular tutorial times with her tutor. They use the progress review forms to identify how the candidate is doing and how she needs to improve. This is a formal method of providing formative assessment.

4. A mature candidate in information technology, attending an open-learning workshop, is very nervous about the idea of getting a qualification. She is given regular formative feedback on her progress with a chance to discuss how she can improve. She is given encouragement to decide when she feels able to cope with a formal assessment.

	Characteristics	**Purpose**
Formative assessment	Ongoing Continuous Feedback for improvement	To diagnose and plan
Summative assessment	Final Summing up achievements at a particular point in time	To describe and accredit

Figure 3.2 *Formative and summative assessment*

Summative

This type of assessment represents a formal 'summing up' of the candidate's achievement at a particular point in time. A candidate could arrange to be officially assessed on a number of elements after receiving a series of formative assessments. This official assessment conducted by an accredited assessor would be a summative assessment of their competence at that time. The results of this assessment would be officially recorded and would serve as a statement of the candidate's competence at the time of the assessment. Other examples of summative assessment include:

- end of year/end of course examinations
- end of unit tests for GNVQs
- the final grade given to completed projects or assignments.

Fair and reliable assessment

As we mentioned in Chapter 1, the candidate is entitled to feel confident that they will be treated fairly when working towards NVQs and GNVQs. This means that there should not be anything preventing them having access to assessment, nor should there be any bias or discrimination during the assessment process.

Access to assessment

Chapter 5 gives some indications of the kind of barriers that might prevent individuals from gaining fair access to assessment. There are many different kinds of problems that people might face and every assessor will have their own examples. Here are a few from our own experience and the measures taken to combat them:

- A candidate in information technology who developed arthritis. A special keyboard overlay was obtained for the computer that helped her to hit the keys accurately.

- A candidate in residential care who could only work on the night shift. An assessor was found who was prepared to conduct an assessment observation during this time.

- A candidate in an engineering firm whose first language was Somalian spoke good enough English to carry out his job. However, he needed help in understanding the details of how he was to be assessed. An interpreter was found who attended the planning interviews to make sure that he was able to understand and discuss anything that was necessary.

- A young girl who had been in care since she was a child was placed on a youth training programme working with animals. She was given a good deal of encouragement and a very slow and gentle introduction to the process of assessment by giving her feedback on an informal basis. When her supervisor was certain she had a good chance of being successful, she suggested that the girl was assessed against one unit of the qualification. Success in this increased the girl's confidence and she was soon able to be assessed against other units.

- A candidate wanting to be assessed for commercial harvesting was told by the assessor where he worked that he would have to wait until June to harvest the strawberries. This is because candidates had *always* been assessed harvesting strawberries. When it was pointed out that it was just as possible to assess the candidate harvesting another type of crop, the assessor realized that the candidate could be assessed almost straight away – harvesting broccoli!

Fairness in assessment

The majority of assessments contain some subjective judgement, particularly when assessment is of more complex skills or knowledge. There are times when a subjective judgement is appropriate, for example, when a candidate asks for a personal opinion of a particular idea, process or product. However, in general, so that assessment is fair, reliable and to national standards, it is important that safeguards are in place to make the summative assessments of NVQs and GNVQs as objective as possible. This can be a problem when working to performance criteria where language such as 'relevant' and 'appropriate' is frequently used. This may lead to subjective interpretations which reflect the personal bias of the assessor, and hence are neither fair to the candidate nor a reliable indicator of a 'national' standard. One major safeguard is for the assessor to check out his or her own interpretation of such woolly terms with other assessors and internal and external verifiers. Some consensus might then arise to curb any subjective excesses.

Another way that subjective judgements can cloud the objectivity of an assessment is in the 'halo' and 'horns' effect where a candidate is considered 'good' or 'poor' by the assessor and all evidence is judged on that basis, as opposed to being judged on its own merit. Probably the most effective safeguard that can operate here is the assessor's own awareness of where he or she might be biased or have personal preferences, plus a strict adherence to the requirements of the elements being assessed.

Unfair discrimination

Both NVQs and GNVQs emphasize good equal opportunities practice, based on equal access to assessment irrespective of age, gender, religion, ethnic group, disability or geographical location. In our experience, many issues that occur related to discrimination seem to do so because of a lack of awareness that they *are* discriminatory.

Knowledge about equal opportunities issues, the policies of their own organizations and the legislation that exists can help those involved in assessment to become more aware of what they need to address. However, just as in the previous section, one of the most powerful means of preventing unfair discrimination is by an open-minded examination of one's own beliefs and prejudices and how they may affect one's judgement. The subject of equal opportunities is far too extensive to be covered here in any detail; however, here are some examples of how discrimination might affect judgement:

- an assessor being prejudiced against someone because they think they are too young to have the required skills, rather than objectively viewing the evidence
- an assessor in child care being particularly hard on a male candidate because the assessor does not think that this is 'man's work' so wants to discourage him
- an assessor undervaluing the practical skills demonstrated by a candidate whose first language is Urdu, because the candidate's command of English is not perfect
- an assessor treating someone in a wheelchair like a child and being over-generous in their assessment.

Some of these may strike a chord in the reader. If not, dig deeper. The majority of people have at least one significant prejudice which could affect their ability to assess fairly.

Methods of assessment

There are a number of assessment methods commonly used in NVQs and GNVQs. This next section considers three of these methods in detail: observation, oral testing and written testing.

Observation: assessing practical competence

This is the main method by which competence is assessed and involves either observation of performance or examination of the end-product. Many people in work will have been involved in informal assessment of performance by observing and making judgements about how effectively someone is doing their job. Teachers or trainers will be used to watching how an individual student or trainee learns or behaves and making mental notes on areas of strength and areas where they may need help. However, candidates for the assessor and verifier awards will need to be able to observe and record on a formal basis.

The person carrying out an observation will need to follow these key points on the observation process:

- be clear about what is being assessed
- ensure that the candidate is clear on this as well
- use a checklist if it helps
- if not familiar with the place, try and visit beforehand
- find the best place to sit or stand during the observation
- try and give the candidate some control over the conditions, eg, ask their opinion on the best place to stand or sit and, if feasible, respect their wishes
- keep out of the eyeline of the person being assessed
- if their work involves interacting with other people, keep out of their eyelines as well
- avoid standing where the candidate needs to move
- when clients are involved, make sure the candidate knows that their needs should come first
- make sure that anyone else involved is reassured about the presence of an observer
- ensure that there is time after the observation to give immediate feedback and discuss what has been observed
- make sure that all Health and Safety requirements eg, footwear are complied with

Example 1: Observation in the workplace
Looking at the floor plan in Figure 3.3, a number of factors would influence where the observer performing the assessment was positioned. If the assessor worked in the salon, then both clients and staff would be used to their presence and hence the assessor might choose to stand right next to the candidate when he or she was working with the client (A1). If the assessor came from outside the salon, their presence would be more noticeable and this would have to be taken into account. If the observation was assessing general client care and service, then the assessor could sit on a seat in the waiting area (B1) and arrange that the candidate always worked in the position nearest to the shop window, ie, the position with client number 1. The assessor could then move to have a final look at the finished 'product' once the client's hair had been styled. However, if the observer was assessing competence in perming hair, then close observation of techniques and

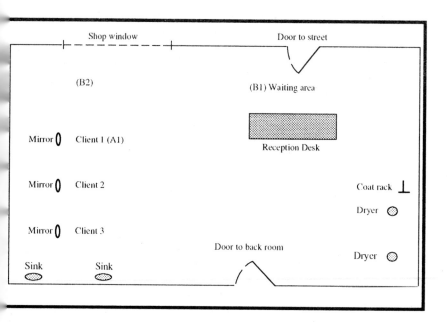

Figure 3.3 *Floor plan of a hairdressing salon*

procedures used would be essential. In this case, the assessor would need to be next to the candidate and, in that situation, would obviously need to decide where they could stand to cause the minimum disruption. There, it would probably be a good idea to ensure that the candidate was not working in the client number 2 position. This would be because the assessor would have to stand in the small space between two sets of clients. Possibly position (B2) might be the least intrusive.

Example 2: Observation of a group working
An assessor for GNVQs or for NVQs in training and development or management might have to conduct an observation of someone conducting a meeting, giving a presentation or running a training session.

The danger here is that the assessor will find themselves physically in the middle of the group which is bound to affect the 'normality' of the situation. Apart from the general points already mentioned, it could be useful to:

- arrive before the group meets and place a chair at the back of the room outside the area where the rest will be sitting
- apart from greeting people briefly and pleasantly if appropriate, try to minimize the conversation with members of the group otherwise the 'dynamics' of the group may be altered

■   avoid too much eye contact

■   use a method of recording the observation that does not involve a lot of noise – in a quiet environment where people are concentrating on what is being discussed, rustling papers can prove disruptive.

In certain circumstances, it may be inappropriate or impossible for the assessor to be present when a candidate is performing a task or carrying out a procedure. In such cases, the use of videotape or possibly audiotape may be admissable evidence.

Questioning: assessing knowledge and understanding across the range

The use of questions, either oral or written, is the main method for establishing whether the candidate has knowledge and understanding across a range of contexts and contingencies. This is vital, as without knowing what exactly they are doing, why, and what the possible alternatives are, there is little possibility that an individual would be able to transfer any skill from one situation to another and instead of the desired highly-skilled and flexible workforce, we would end up with a nation of robots.

There are limits to what an observation can tell the assessor about how much someone actually knows what they are doing. An observation is at a particular time and place, in a particular environment, under a particular set of circumstances. For example, the assessor could observe someone using a computer, but may not be able to tell whether that person could cope if a fault appeared in the program or if they were working on a different type of computer or if they were working in a busy environment with a lot of time pressure. Well-constructed and relevant questioning can find out this information from the candidate. In Chapter 9, there is a more detailed explanation of how different testing methods suit particular work contexts. However, it is obviously important to choose questioning methods appropriate to the activity being tested. The next section will consider the different types of oral questions and written tests that can be used.

Open and closed questions

Broadly speaking, questions can be divided into the categories of 'open' or 'closed' types which have distinctive features and functions. Open questions, associated with prompt words such as 'How?' and 'Why?' offer the opportunity for the candidate to respond fully and in their own words. Closed questions are associated with phrases such as 'Do you think...?' where the candidate can only respond with 'Yes' or 'No', and with prompt words such as 'What?' and 'Where?' when the candidate is required to respond with specific factual information.

Choosing the right type of question

The assessor needs to be clear on why they are asking the question and what

Function	Example
Set at ease	'Would you like a coffee?'
	'What sort of journey have you had?'
Ask for general information	'What were your responsibilities as ...?'
	'What have you been doing in the past year?'
Ask for specific information	'What is your name?'
	'How do you save data on a disk?'
	'Precisely what does that entail?'
Ask for further information	'Could you tell me some more about that?'
	'Can you give me some more details?'
Identify agreement or disagreement	'Do you think he acted correctly?'
	'Did you agree with the way she dealt with that situation?'
Ask the reason or justification	'Can you tell me why you used that particular technique?'
	'Why is ice put in the glass before pouring the drink?'
Ask for opinions, ideas	'What do you think of this product?'
	'Do you believe in positive discrimination?'

Figure 3.4 *Different functions of questions*

answer or answers will be acceptable. When testing knowledge and understanding at levels 1 or 2, it is likely that questions will be simple and closed because specific factual knowledge is being tested. For example, at NVQ level 2 in construction, a candidate might be asked to give five examples of construction work that would need to be protected against the weather while other work was being finished. The assessor will have a list of acceptable answers and will accept any five of these answers from the candidate. Some more open questions may also be appropriate, for example asking the candidate 'Why?' they are using a particular process or piece of equipment. It is likely that the answers to these questions would be fairly short and simple. At level 5, the question and answer process will inevitably become far more complex. For example, to assess knowledge and understanding of principles and methods of defining and allocating responsibilities and authority would probably require a variety of different types of questioning and involve both oral and written answers.

Oral questioning
In a large number of work contexts it is likely that the testing of knowledge and understanding in NVQs will be oral rather than written. In order to carry out an oral assessment, the assessor needs a bank of questions from which to choose. In Chapter 11, there are samples from a bank of questions that could be used with candidates for the assessor awards.

An assessor could ask questions at appropriate times during an observation or set aside a separate time after the observation to ask all the questions together. Alternatively, the assessor may choose to question knowledge and understanding across the range when the full portfolio of evidence is being assessed. These decisions can only be made by the assessor in discussion with the candidate. However, the person asking the questions should take the individual needs of each candidate into account.

PUTTING THE CANDIDATE AT EASE It goes without saying that the candidate is likely to be nervous and the assessor needs to be sensitive to this. The more confident the candidate feels, the more likely they will be able to give a true representation of what they really know. It usually helps if the candidate actually knows what the procedure will be, that they can ask for a question to be repeated and that they can take their time answering.

ENSURING THE LANGUAGE IS AT THE RIGHT LEVEL AND CAN BE UNDERSTOOD Be clear as to what is being tested and avoid using over-complex language if this is not necessary. Be aware of what the candidate's normal range of vocabulary is likely to be and take that into account when phrasing questions. Distinguish between essential technical jargon that they will need in their vocational area and inessential use of over-sophisticated vocabulary.

NOT ASKING LEADING QUESTIONS The assessor should be careful not to use questions that could lead the candidate by giving them a clue to the right answer. They should also be aware of any preferences or opinions they might hold which could affect the way they ask questions. It is just as easy to lead the candidate by the tone or inflection of voice or by some facial expression or body movement. One assessor we know would automatically purse her lips and lean forward slightly if the answer she was getting was incorrect. However difficult it may be, a neutral but pleasant expression is the ideal!

- Your client seemed a bit uncomfortable, didn't she?
- Don't you think you should have cleaned the floor before the woodwork?
- Why would you say UVPC was better than wood?

Figure 3.5 *Examples of leading questions*

Written testing

There are a number of different types of written testing used within NVQs and GNVQs and the choice of the appropriate test form depends entirely on what level and complexity of knowledge and understanding need to be demonstrated. The main ones are:

Yes/No or True/False responses	A statement is followed by either a Yes/No or True/False response to be ticked or circled. *Example: A larch tree is an evergreen True/False.*
Objective tests (multiple choice)	A question is asked followed by several alternatives, out of which one must be selected. *Example: A chronological filing system is one where files are arranged according to:* *a) geographical area* *b) initial letter of surname* *c) date received* *d) reference number.*
Gapped statements	A statement or longer piece of text with a space or spaces left for the candidate to complete. *Example: Foods which are high in fibre include.......... and ....* NB. sometimes the candidate is free to write any appropriate word and sometimes the word or words can be selected from a given list.
Short answer tests	A series of questions which require answers of a few words or a few lines. *Example: Explain briefly how a colour correction filter works.*
Essays	Set topics, usually with a defined number of words, often involving research through reading and including the structuring and development of ideas. *Example: Discuss how different learning theories can be used in planning training programmes.*
Reports	Set subject with clearly defined objectives based on practical research and laid out with headings following a conventional report structure.

Example: Write a report on the procedures for employee appraisal within your organization with recommendations for improvement.

Assignments/projects Set topics usually entailing some practical research and written explanation and analysis of what has been discovered.

Example: Choose one specific client group in the community, eg, young mothers, pensioners' etc. Find out what services are provided for them and their opinion of these services. Compare local to national provision. Present your information using both written and visual means.

Difficulties in assessing knowledge and understanding

All of the methods above can test knowledge from a simple to a sophisticated level, however, it is evident that those requiring more complex responses will be far more useful in establishing whether the candidate actually understands the knowledge they are demonstrating.

The more complex the activity the greater possibility there is of generating evidence against a variety of different elements and the more opportunity there is for demonstration of other skills. The assignment given in the example above would enable GNVQ candidates to demonstrate a variety of core skills including *communication, working with others* and *problem solving.* If it involved analysis of data, they could also cover *application of number* and if the results were produced using a computer, then *information technology* would also be covered. However there are a number of difficulties in the assessment of knowledge and understanding:

- The assessor has to make a decision on how much knowledge and understanding can be inferred from what a candidate is doing or what they have produced. Sometimes this is straightforward, particularly if the assessor is in regular contact with the candidate and has observed a number of times covering a range of situations and contexts. However, sometimes this could be misleading, eg, assuming that a trainer being assessed 'knows' about different learning theories, because they have used a number of different teaching methods.

- The more complex methods of testing knowledge such as essays also pose difficulties for the assessor. The material produced by the candidate is more individualized and there are far more information and ideas to disentangle, hence the demands on the assessor to have very clear ideas of what will or will not be acceptable and what is or is not relevant are far greater. This has obvious advantages, in that candidates have a full opportunity to express themselves if appropriate. However, the potential for subjective and unfair assessments can be considerable.

■ There is sometimes a problem in being sure about the depth of knowledge to be demonstrated and it can be difficult to gauge this from reading the standards. There is no easy answer here and guidance should be obtained by consulting with external verifiers and ensuring consistency of understanding and practice between assessors. However, it is possible to form some idea of the depth of knowledge required by referring to the description of the level of qualification, eg, NVQ level 1 refers to *routine and predictable work activities*, whereas level 5 refers to a *significant range of fundamental principles across a wide and often unpredictable range of contexts.*

■ The limitations of testing knowledge in relation to specific elements rather than covering larger inter-related areas is also seen as problematic by some assessors. This can be an issue if knowledge at all levels is treated in an over-simplistic way. However, it is important to remember here that a substantial piece of evidence could be cross-referenced so that it provides proof of knowledge and understanding across a whole group of elements. It is up to those advising and assessing to help candidates to realize this where appropriate.

Skills with people

Good assessment is about people as well as standards. In the assessment of NVQs and GNVQs there are some areas where no negotiation is possible. It is the assessor's judgement which determines whether an individual has met the requirements of the elements being assessed and, as long as the assessor's judgement is fair and reliable, there should be no argument. However, the fairness and reliability of this judgement can be affected by not taking into account the characteristics of the candidate and the situation in which they are working. Let us look at four different candidates and mention briefly possible considerations in the approach to assessment.

■ *NVQ level 1 – amenity horticulture*
The candidate has learning difficulties and a tendency to get worked up under pressure. However, he has shown a real aptitude for gardening and could hold down a regular job.
– Assessor should try to be friendly and natural, making as little of the assessment process as possible in order to give the candidate the best chance of demonstrating his ability.

■ *NVQ level 3 – care (terminal care)*
The candidate has worked for a number of years in voluntary service where she held a position of some responsibility. She then began work in a hospice where she is dealing with patients sympathetically and

effectively.

– Assessor would need to be aware of the sensitivity of the situation and may consider it appropriate to take the lead from the candidate about how to carry out the assessment. In particular, the feelings of the patients would need to be a major consideration.

- *GNVQ level 2 – health and social care*
  The candidate is 15 years old and working towards this qualification at school.
  – Assessor will probably be a teacher at school and might also be using the assessment to monitor the student's general progress and response to the programme. In this situation, the assessor would probably liaise with other assessors to compare judgements on progress in order that the feedback to the student could be as informed as possible.
- *NVQ level 5 – management*
  The candidate is a senior manager in a local authority.
  – At this level the assessor would expect that the candidate should be well used to pressure and responsibility. Possibly the main consideration would be to keep as much out of the way as possible and ensure that the assessment does not take more time than is strictly necessary.

Anyone assessing or advising on NVQs or GNVQs will be dealing with a variety of different candidates, all with their own characteristics and particular needs, who are not just having assessment 'done' to them but who are encouraged to take an active part in the assessment process. Some candidates may find this easy and, after the initial briefing, will get the idea of what is required and be quite happy to take a proactive role. Many candidates will not find it so easy and will view their possible involvement with suspicion, and perhaps trepidation. The adviser or assessor may find this a tricky situation and may be tempted to take one of two extreme approaches. One approach might be to abdicate all responsibility and tell the candidate it is up to them to plan for assessment and for the collection of evidence. The other approach might be to take on a highly directive role and tell the candidate exactly what they think they should do. In some cases, the failure of the first approach might lead the adviser or assessor to fall back on the second. The skill for the adviser or assessor is to do neither, but to weigh up the amount of support and guidance appropriate for each candidate at each stage in working towards the qualification. Some hints on this:

- avoid giving too much responsibility too soon as this could inhibit some candidates by making them feel overwhelmed
- with inexperienced candidates, help them to make choices by the use of structured alternatives eg, 'Would you prefer...or...?'
- always give them the opportunity to make suggestions
- avoid immediately rejecting suggestions made by candidates
- explore disagreements rather than impose your own point of view

1)	**Let the Candidate Have the First Say**
	Give them the chance to say how they think they have done. If they haven't achieved competence it is possible they will be able to identify why and this will help them to 'own' the feedback they receive.
2)	**Give Praise Before Criticism**
	Most people will find it difficult to try to improve if they feel they are a failure. By focusing first on their strengths and then helping them to recognize their weaker areas, you can give the candidate enough confidence to deal with what went wrong.
3)	**Limit What You Cover**
	Don't try to cover everything. Focus on two or three key areas for development.
4)	**Be Specific, Not Vague**
	Try to avoid general comments which don't help the candidate to identify the problem. It's not very useful to say to someone 'Your writing isn't very good'. It's much more useful to say, 'It was difficult to read what you had written, because your writing is rather small and you crowded all your information together without leaving any spaces in between the different sections'.
5)	**Concentrate on Things That Can Be Changed**
	For feedback to be useful it must allow for the possibility of improvement. If there are intrinsic or extrinsic factors which you know cannot be changed, the feedback relating to this is a waste of time. It is far more useful to concentrate on what can be changed.
6)	**Give the Candidate Time to Think and Respond**
	Successful feedback involves a 'dialogue' between two individuals committed to improvement. If you've given the candidate a new perspective on some aspect of competence it could take some time for them to absorb. Only when they have absorbed it and then responded can the planning for improvement take place.
7)	**Keep to the Standards**
	As assessor/adviser you must distinguish between when the candidate has done something different from how you would do it but has still met the standards and when they have not performed to the required level of competence. You might draw their attention to this difference but be clear as to whether it is acceptable in relation to the standards or not.
8)	**Make Sure They Understand**
	Think of the language you are using and ensure it is the right level and tone.
9)	**Listen to How the Feedback is Received**
	Be aware of how the candidate is reacting to your feedback. Look for non-verbal cues that they are confused or that they don't agree.
10)	**End on a Positive Note**
	End the feedback session agreeing some positive action that can be taken to address any areas for development that have been identified. End with some encouragement as well!

Figure 3.6 *Points to consider when giving feedback*

- be clear yourself on what you can negotiate and what you cannot
- make it clear to candidates what can or cannot be negotiated
- if candidates refuse to accept your advice, consider this carefully
- if you are blocking their right to choose, think again
- if, by not taking your advice, they will not produce appropriate evidence, make this clear.

Skills in giving feedback

A number of skills related to working with people have already been mentioned. However, there is one key skill at the heart of assessment – the skill of giving constructive and helpful feedback. If this skill is used, the candidate will not just be clear on what they have achieved, they will be clear on what they need to do to develop. They will also be motivated by the feedback to try and improve on their performance.

It might be an assessor who has to give feedback to the candidate, an APL adviser discussing a candidate's first attempt at a portfolio of evidence, or an internal verifier monitoring work colleagues acting as assessors. In every case, the effect of badly delivered feedback can destroy confidence and trust. This is particularly important if the candidate has not been able to demonstrate competence or achievement and might be tempted to give up and not try again. The main skills involved are based on the idea of respect for individuals, involvement of individuals in the assessment process and a sensitivity to how the other person is responding to what is being said.

Summary

This chapter you should have helped you with the following:

- different types of assessment
- different methods of assessment
- skills in observation and questioning
- skills with people
- skills in giving feedback.

4 Awarding Bodies, Quality Assurance and Approved Centres

The role of lead and awarding bodies in the development of national standards; the role and function of awarding bodies in assessor/verifier accreditation; the Common Accord and quality assurance; selecting the appropriate awards; choosing a centre.

This chapter explains the role and functions of the key bodies involved with the assessor/verifier/APL adviser awards, gives information on the national occupational standards and qualifications system, and discusses the importance of quality assurance and the importance of the Common Accord. This is followed by guidance on the selection of awards and centres.

The role of lead and awarding bodies in the development of national standards

Occupational areas

There are 11 occupational areas within the NVQ framework. Each of these areas has one or more lead bodies amongst whose functions is that of supervising the development and any subsequent revisions of national standards designed to achieve competent performance. Membership of lead bodies comprises representation from the public sector, from industry, professional bodies, employer and trades associations and practitioners. The Training and Development Lead Body (TDLB) is the Industry Lead Body (ILB) for the occupational area designated as 'Developing and extending knowledge and skill'. The TDLB has defined the key purpose of training and development as being 'To develop human potential to assist organizations and individuals to achieve their objectives'. Standards for training and development were first issued in 1992, the revised version being published in 1995. All national standards are linked to job roles; those for training and development are related to the stages of the training cycle, as explained in Chapter 1. Everyone involved in assessing NVQs or GNVQs now needs to be competent not only in their vocational area, eg, manufacturing, tending animals, plants and land or providing business services, but also in the skills and knowledge related to advising, assessing and verifying. The assessor, verifier and adviser awards have been devised to enable all assessors to be credited with the necessary competences without having to take a full NVQ in training and development. These awards are units from a particular section of the standards related to the assessment of competence, as shown in Figure 4.1.

OCCUPATIONAL AREA - DEVELOPING AND EXTENDING KNOWLEDGE AND SKILL

Vocational Area: Training and Development

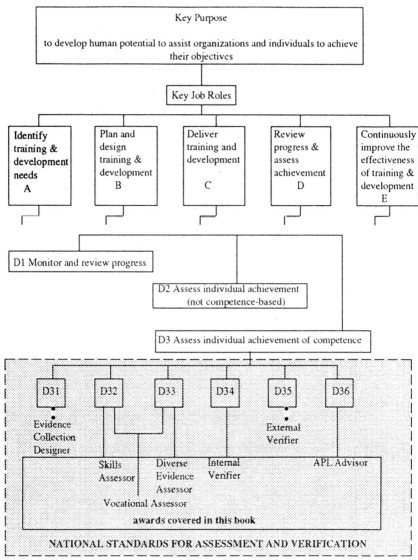

Figure 4.1 *The relationship of the assessor, verifier and adviser awards to the national standards for Training and Development*

Qualifications framework

Once standards have been developed and approved by the lead bodies, they are formed into qualifications by awarding bodies which are accredited by NCVQ to offer NVQs. (See the glossary for clarification of these terms.) All NVQ qualifications developed from standards devised by the TDLB and any of the other lead bodies need to be approved by NCVQ to ensure that they fit into the overall qualifications framework at the appropriate levels. This framework is a national system for ordering NVQs according to the complexity of job roles. There are five levels in all. NVQs in training and development are all at level 3 or above.

Level 1 – competence which involves the application of knowledge in the performance of a range of varied work activities, most of which may be routine or predictable.

Level 2 – competence which involves the application of knowledge in a significant range of varied work activities, performed in a variety of contexts. Some of the activities are complex or non-routine, and there is some individual responsibility or autonomy. Collaboration with others, perhaps through membership of a work group or team, may often be a requirement.

Level 3 – competence which involves the application of knowledge in a broad range of varied work activities performed in a wide variety of contexts, most of which are complex and non-routine. There is considerable responsibility and autonomy, and control and guidance of others is often required.

Level 4 – competence which involves the application of knowledge in a broad range of complex technical or professional work activities performed in a wide variety of contexts and with a substantial degree of personal responsibility and autonomy. Responsibility for the work of others and the allocation of resources is often present.

Level 5 – competence which involves the application of a significant range of fundamental principles across a wide and often unpredictable variety of contexts. Very substantial personal autonomy, and often significant responsibility for the work of others and for the allocation of substantial resources feature strongly, as do personal accountabilities for analysis and diagnosis, design, planning, execution and evaluation.

So far, there are NVQs at level 5 only in management, although level 5 in training and development is currently being revised.

GNVQ levels are described as foundation (formerly level 1), intermediate (formerly level 2) and advanced (formerly level 3). Figure 4.2 gives an overview of the broad qualifications framework.

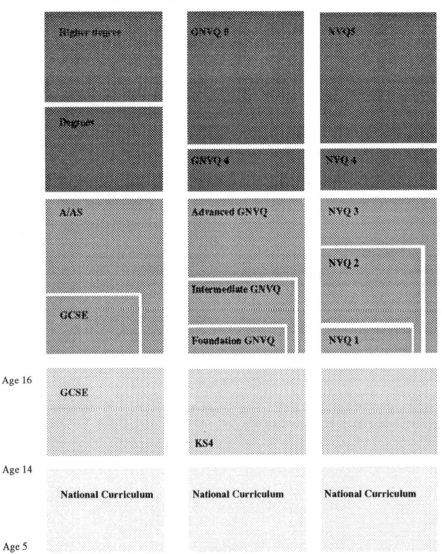

Figure 4.2 *A mapping of current qualifications (as attempted by NCVQ)*

Awarding bodies involved in assessor/verifier accreditation

Within each occupational area there are awarding bodies whose prime functions are to set procedures, devise qualifications and assessments, monitor centres, assess results and provide awards, supply training for assessors, verifiers and moderators, and produce publications. When the TDLB standards were first published, NCVQ accredited the five English awarding bodies connected with generic training, ie, CGLI, RSA, BTEC, ITD (to be known as the Institute of Personnel and Development) and PEI to offer the assessor/verifier/adviser awards. In Scotland, SCOTVEC (Scottish Vocational Education Council) is the sole awarding body. Once the standards for each occupational area have been approved, the awarding bodies devised NVQs at the appropriate levels, together with appropriate documentation and guidance, and in some cases materials to support personal development or give a greater understanding of the knowledge elements required. While the NVQs and the assessor and verifier awards devised by awarding bodies were based on exactly the same standards, the actual packages marketed and sold to candidates differed quite markedly in terms of approach, design, presentation and cost.

Choosing an awarding body

Candidates sometimes ask us which is the 'best' awarding body to register with, and this indicates that in the public mind there is still some sort of perceived hierarchy or status that attaches to qualifications awarded by particular bodies. Many candidates will now be encouraged to take their assessor awards through the ILB related to their profession, eg, the Institute of the Motor Industry (IMI), or EnTra (Engineering Training Authority); many candidates are still likely to choose one of the generic training bodies mentioned earlier. Apart from 'perceived status', most candidates choose their awarding body on a combination of product and cost factors. There have been a number of comparative studies done between the services and materials provided, and these indicate that each awarding body has different strengths and appeal. Professional trainers, interested in continuous professional development, for example, may prefer to take their awards through the Institute of Personnel and Development which is also one of the professional organizations for trainers, and whose process for the awards encourages reflective learning. City and Guilds, who in the recent past has offered a number of qualifications containing assessment components, (eg, 924-6-9 series) has produced initial self-assessment guides to assist candidates who may be able to claim through APL. A comprehensive training day is offered by the RSA, and its materials contain information on the required underpinning knowledge and understanding. BTEC has developed some examples of indexing evidence, and a user-friendly guide to the interpretation of the different elements. A complete list of awarding bodies offering assessor and verifier qualifications can be found in *NVQ Monitor*, the quarterly magazine produced by NCVQ.

The Common Accord and quality assurance

Inevitably, as the number of approved centres offering awards, designated and qualified assessors, and candidates for awards increased, there was a growth in differences of opinion and sometimes in practice between centres and advice offered to candidates which was unhelpful. In August 1993, the NCVQ adopted the Common Accord, which is 'intended to enhance the quality and cost effectiveness of NVQ assessment and verification processes operated by awarding bodies' (NCVQ, 1993). The Accord was developed by the NCVQ and by, amongst others, the main awarding bodies participating in the assessment of NVQs. The main features of the Accord are:

- common terminology to describe the roles of individuals and organizations in the assessment and quality assurance system
- certification to national standards for assessors and verifiers
- defined roles in quality assurance for both awarding bodies and the organizations which they approve to offer NVQs
- explicit criteria for approving organizations to offer NVQs
- quality assurance and control systems to ensure rigour and monitor equal opportunities implementation.

All approved centres should have a copy of the Common Accord, which can also be obtained from NCVQ. Since 1993 there has been a steady growth in the number of awarding bodies accredited to offer single units of credit, eg D 32 'Assess natural performance', irrespective of whether the awarding body is running programmes in, or offering, full NVQs in training and development. This has meant that awarding bodies from all vocational areas offering NVQ's have moved from running 'assessment preparation' sessions to delivering, assessing and accrediting the assessor and verifier awards themselves, thus enabling designated assessors, internal verifiers and APL advisers to gain credit for competence as quickly as possible. The Common Accord has laid down the *minimum* requirements for each assessment function, ie, assessor – D32 and/or D33, internal verifier – D34, external verifier – D35 (verifiers will eventually need D32 and D33 as well) and suggests that existing centres should have staff qualified to these minimum standards by 1995. Only staff involved in the *assessment and verification* of NVQs will need to take the awards; this may mean that some organizations will completely separate out the assessment function from that of delivery (unusual until now in, for example, schools and colleges) and indeed, there are now assessment and accreditation centres whose only function is to provide assessment for NVQs. Small organizations may need or want to have the same person doing both training and assessment and use an internal verifier from another organization.

The context of assessment and verification work

Various full NVQs in different vocational areas contain the unit D32 'Assess candidate performance' as an integral part of the qualification. The Common Accord guarantees that all awarding bodies must accept each others' awards, eg, an assessor who has gained their D32/33 through RSA can use it to assess

BTEC GNVQs. However, it is desirable that those responsible for assessing TDLB units in a *training* context should have an understanding of training and development as a vocational area, as well as competence in their own vocational area. An example would be a bricklayer highly competent in all practical aspects of her or his craft, but who had never undertaken training or supervision of others in any extensive way. If this bricklayer were asked to start to supervise and assess the training skills of other staff, she or he would ideally gain experience in training, supervising and assessing, and be working towards units from other areas of the TDLB awards, as well as D32/33, before undertaking any assessment function in the context of training others.

The role of the verifiers is crucial in quality assurance for the system. External verifiers will need to prepare reports for awarding bodies based on their monitoring visits; they will rely a great deal on the internal verifiers of approved centres to maintain standards and ensure that procedures and practices for assessment are being implemented. NCVQ will receive consolidated reports from awarding bodies.

The Common Accord relates to the assessment and verification of NVQs. A similar document will deal with assessment and verification issues relating to GNVQs.

Selecting the appropriate awards

Since the five levels of NVQs are all related to job role, a candidate can take an NVQ at a higher level only if their job role matches the requirements of the NVQ units at that level. Otherwise, candidates can 'progress' by acquiring and practising more skills identified in units of the same level. It is essential to be really clear about this relationship between current job roles and NVQ units. As far as the assessor/ verifier/adviser awards are concerned, there has been such an emphasis on the *delivery* of training, rather than its assessment, that many find it difficult to understand that they need to focus on the assessment process as a separate yet integral part of their work. This sometimes leads to a failure to differentiate between presenting evidence supporting delivery (eg, presentation skills, planning) and that supporting assessment. A common misunderstanding is that the numbers associated with units represent some sort of progression, eg, that D36 is 'higher' than D32. This is *not* the case with any NVQ units, which are based on an analysis of job role or task. Instead, the candidate has to decide whether an individual unit represents an activity in which they are currently engaged and it is this that forms the basis for the choice of award. If a candidate's assessment role is to assess natural performance in the workplace or in simulated environments, and they do not make assessments about candidates on any other grounds, then only D32, 'Assess candidate's natural performance' will be required. Likewise, if the role is specifically to advise candidates *before* assessment, D36 would be needed. It is only worthwhile registering for an award which represents a job role *not* being currently undertaken if the candidate wants to gain or demonstrate the acquisition of underpinning knowledge and understanding *prior* to practical activity.

Choosing a centre

All awards are certificated through centres, (or in the case of the RSA, registered assessors, who may be freelance or attached to a centre), which are approved by various awarding bodies to assess and accredit candidates and, in the case of larger organizations, to provide advice, guidance and training as well. These centres are often known as Assessment and Accreditation centres (AACs) or Assessment, Delivery and Accreditation centres (ADACs). There are clear criteria laid down in the Common Accord for the approval of centres. A centre may have several sites all operating under the same systems. Centres may choose to register with one or any number of awarding bodies offering the assessor/verifier/adviser awards, which may of course be the deciding factor in choice for candidates. Awarding bodies will be pleased to supply lists of registered centres and, in the case of the RSA, registered assessors.

Services

Centres deal with candidate registrations, allocation of candidates to assessors, assessment and certification paperwork, and usually any associated support needed by candidates. Many offer the facility for accrediting prior learning. Probably the biggest factor in a candidate's ability to profit fully from the process associated with gaining an award is the variety and quality of the training, support and assessment offered by the centre with which they register. It would be wise to check the range of supporting materials in the centre such as books and journals relating to assessment. Most produce a variety of backup materials to supplement those provided by the awarding bodies and NCVQ. (Refer to the suggestions for further reading at the back of the book for an idea of publications that are available for added support.) It is also important to check that the service offered is right for the staff or organization concerned before making a final decision to register. The list below gives an idea of the range of services that can be offered by approved centres:

- briefing sessions – introducing the awards and the NVQ system
- portfolio workshops – guiding candidates in the collection of evidence
- knowledge and understanding workshops – training in background information
- open learning – materials that can be studied at the candidate's convenience

- individual support – tutorials on a one-to-one basis
- group support – either tutored sessions or self-support groups
- workplace assessment – assessors visit the real work environment to assess
- simulated work environments – provision of practice space and equipment
- accreditation of prior learning – staff trained to check this and provide action plans.

Costs

Timescale and cost are difficult to estimate, because they depend on the individual awarding body's charges, the rates charged by different centres, the amount of support required by individuals, and the ability of the staff providing the support, training and assessment. Some candidates have taken as little as three weeks to provide sufficient evidence for successful assessment, whereas others have taken months. On average, we have found that a candidate assessor who is new to NVQ/GNVQ assessment requires about 15 hours of training/support and about five hours of assessment (workplace and portfolio combined) to achieve D32 and D33. Motivation, an overall grasp of the assessment system in use and opportunities for assessment are the keys to fast accreditation (see chapter 9 for more details of assessment in different work contexts).

Costs incurred will be of both variable and fixed types, depending on whether they relate to 'products' such as certification, or processes, such as assessment time. These will vary according to the procedures of the awarding body and the assessment centre selected. Some of the expenses incurred by centres such as centre approval fees, are likely to be passed on to candidates in some way. Costs can sometimes be kept down by attending group sessions rather than one-to-one sessions; candidates will have to consider whether the financial saving is worth the loss of individual tuition and support. An often hidden cost is that of the time spent by the candidate, frequently in non-work time, in preparing for the assessment. Charges related to assessment will include all or some of the following:

- centre approval and registration
- candidate registration (per unit or award)
- support materials, candidate packs
- support workshops
- workplace assessment
- portfolio assessment
- internal and external verification
- administration and travel costs.

It may well be that potential candidates already work for an organization accredited to offer the awards, in which case they may or may not have a choice of approved centre. Some organizations will prefer to choose centres which offer awards through awarding bodies which correspond with the work of staff who will be undertaking the awards, eg, IPD awards for staff working on IPD programmes, whereas others will want to choose one awarding body for all their staff, irrespective of the programmes delivered and assessed by their staff. Yet others will choose a centre they feel happy with, irrespective of any other factors. Cost, future marketing opportunities and internal quality are all issues which will result from whatever choice is made; 'shopping around' to find the most appropriate package is recommended both for individuals and for organizations.

Summary

This chapter should have helped you with the following:

- understanding the role of ILBs and awarding bodies
- knowing the main details of the Common Accord and the importance of quality assurance
- recognizing that all awarding body standards are identical, with differences being in costs, materials, documentation, support services and assessment procedures
- knowing what questions to ask when selecting an awarding body and an assessment centre
- selecting the appropriate award.

Section 2

How to use the step-by-step guides

Assessment is a holistic, not a fragmented process, and the way that you naturally assess will probably take you through all the stages of the processes that have been identified in the National Standards. For example, if you were planning to assess someone's skills, you would want to:

- plan the assessment with them, identifying what would be assessed
- watch them doing the required tasks
- ask questions so that you were satisfied that their skill rested on a firm base of knowledge and understanding
- let them know whether they were successful
- give them feedback, and
- record the process in some way.

The standards take this process that most assessors have always used, and have broken down the process into tasks (elements). The actual detail of the way in which each of the tasks should be performed is described in the performance criteria for each element. Let us emphasize that we are *not* suggesting that you produce a separate piece of evidence for each criterion. In fact, NCVQ very clearly states, 'It is not appropriate for a separate piece of evidence to be generated for each individual performance criterion. Not only is "atomised" evidence of this sort inefficient, it is also often wrong. It only shows that the candidate achieves the standard on a piecemeal basis, rather than being consistently competent to the full national standard'.

However, we have found that people have had difficulty in interpreting performance criteria, and it is for this reason that we have prepared these guides to take you step by step through the criteria, showing what in particular you need to prove.

Each guide will give you:

- a clear explanation of each performance criterion
- a set of key points to consider about your current practice in assessment/verification/advice
- a grid at the beginning of each element which provides a full list of the performance criteria and range for that element and maps the original standards for assessment (pre-Summer 1994) with the revised version of the standards (post-Summer 1994).

Finding your way through the guides

Each performance criterion is followed by an explanation of what it means and some key points to highlight what you should demonstrate at some point in your evidence or supporting statements related to the units. We have also tried to include useful examples of different situations across the range. However, you should make sure that the full range is covered in your evidence.

Original and revised standards for assessment

The standards have undergone a review during 1994 and at present candidates for the awards may be working to the old standards or preparing to work on the new standards. Do not worry if you have already started working to the old standards; there will be a considerable changeover period and your award will still be valid. The information contained in this book should still provide you with all you need to know.

Comparison of original and revised standards

In the following step-by-step guides, we have used the new standards. We have also provided a mapping grid at the beginning of each unit, so that you can see clearly how the two sets compare. We have placed identical or similar criteria opposite one another on the grid. Where there is no similar criterion, a blank space has been left in the appropriate column.

If you look closely at the two sets of standards, you will find that the revised standards sometimes feature identical criteria to the old standards (although the range may have been altered). In a lot of cases, the criteria are quite similar, but the new standards have widened the scope of what is covered or clarified its purpose more specifically.

Information for candidates using the original standards

Virtually all the original performance criteria can be identified in some way as matching similar revised performance criteria. Since there is a degree of commonality between the two sets of standards, we have ensured that the written explanations to performance criteria are adequate for either set of standards. There are only a couple of instances where a performance criterion from the original standards has no counterpart, and we have indicated these explanations clearly in the text. There have been alterations in the knowledge and understanding components of the revised standards, and also in the evidence requirements, so if you are using the step-by-step guides to help you clarify or structure the collection of evidence, doublecheck the specific requirements for the set of standards from which you are working. You should be able to find reference to all necessary knowledge and understanding requirements in the book.

The glossary contains explanations of all essential terms used in the original standards.

A final point

Before you begin, remember that the person who is assessing you for these awards should also be displaying all the competences in assessment that have been identified. This means they should be encouraging you to discuss and ask for clarification on any points which confuse you. **Make sure they do their job!**

Unit D32	**Original (Pre-Summer 1994)** **Assess Candidate Performance**		**Revised (Post-Summer 1994)** **Assess Candidate Performance**
Element D321	*Identify opportunities for the collection of evidence of competent performance*		*Agree and review a plan for assessing performance*
a	the opportunites identified are relevant to the element(s) to be assessed	a	the opportunities identified are relevant to the elements to be assessed
b	best use is made of naturally occurring evidence and related questioning before alternatives are considered	b	best use is made of naturally occurring evidence and related questioning
c	advice is sought when alternative evidence is proposed		
d	opportunities are selected to minimize disruption to normal activity	c	opportunities are selected to minimise disruption to normal activity
e	opportunities are selected to ensure access to fair and reliable assessment	d	opportunities are selected which provide access to fair and reliable assessment
		e	when simulations are proposed, accurate information and advice is sought about their validity and administration
f	a resulting assessment plan is discussed and agreed with candidate and others who may be affected	f	the proposed assessment plan is discussed and agreed with the candidate and others who may be affected
		g	if there is disagreement with the proposed assessment plan, options open to the candidate are explained clearly and constructively
		h	the assessment plan specifies the target elements of competence, the types of evidence to be collected, the assessment methods, the timing of assessments and the arrangements for reviewing progress against the plan
		i	plans are reviewed and updated at agreed times to reflect the candidate's progress within the qualification
	Range *Source of evidence:* natural performance; oral testing; written testing *Context:* normal work; within training programme		**Range** *1. Evidence:* performance evidence; knowledge evidence *2. Evidence derived from:* Examination of products; observations of process; responses to questions *3. Opportunities for evidence collection:* naturally occurring; pre-set simulations and tests; For candidates with special assessment requirements

Element D322	Original (Pre-Summer 1994) *Collect and judge performance evidence against criteria*		Revised (Post-Summer 1994) *Collect and judge performance evidence against criteria*
a	candidate is encouraged to identify and present relevant evidence	a	advice and encouragement to collect evidence efficiently is appropriate to the candidate's needs.
		b	access to assessment is appropriate to the candidate's needs
c	only the specified performance criteria are used in assessments	c	only the performance criteria specified for the element of competence are used to judge the evidence
b	candidate performance is accurately assessed against elements and performance criteria	d	evidence is judged accurately against all the relevant performance criteria
d	the evidence can be attributed to the candidate	e	the evidence is valid and can be attributed to the candidate
e	any pre-set simulations and tests are correctly administered	f	any pre-set simulations and tests are administered correctly
f	the assessor is as unobtrusive as is practicable whilst observing the candidate	g	the assessor is as unobtrusive as is practicable whilst observing the candidate
		h	evidence is judged fairly and reliably
g	difficulties in interpreting performance criteria are referred promptly and accurately to an appropriate authority	i	difficulties in judging evidence fairly and reliably are referred promptly to an appropriate authority
		j	the candidate is given clear and constructive feedback and advice following the judgement
	Range *Sources of evidence:* natural performance; simulations *Type of evidence:* observational; examination of product		**Range** *performance evidence assessed by:* examination of products; observations of process *Candidates:* experienced in presenting evidence; inexperienced in presenting evidence; candidates with special assessment requirements

	Original (Pre-Summer 1994)		Revised (Post-Summer 1994)
Element D323	*Collect and judge knowledge evidence to support the inference of competent performance*		*Collect and judge knowledge evidence*
		a	knowledge relevant to the element is identified accurately from the performance evidence
a	questions are selected to provide sufficient evidence to infer competent performance across the range	b	evidence of knowledge is collected when performance evidence does not cover fully the specified range or contingencies
b	questions are justifiable in relation to potential performance	c	valid methods are used to collect knowledge evidence
c	the inferences of competent performance can be justified		
d	pre-set tests are correctly administered		
e	questions used are clear and do not lead candidates	d	when questions are used, they are clear and do not lead candidates
f	appropriate arrangements are made to maximize access for the candidate according to needs	e	access to assessment is appropriate to the candidate's needs
		f	the knowledge evidence conforms with the content of the knowledge specification and is judged accurately against all the relevant performance criteria
		g	evidence is judged fairly and reliably
		h	difficulties in judging evidence fairly and reliably are referred promptly to an appropriate authority
		i	the candidate is given clear and constructive feedback and advice following the judgement
	Range		**Range**
	Sources of evidence: oral questions; written questions; pre-set questions; assessor-devised questions		*1. Knowledge evidence derived from:* examination of product(s); observation(s) of process; responses to questions *2. Candidates:* experienced in presenting evidence; inexperienced in presenting evidence; Candidates with special assessment requirements *3. Questions:* oral; written; Pre-set questions; assessor-devised questions

	Original (Pre-Summer 1994)		Revised (Post-Summer 1994)
Element D324	*Make assessment decision and provide feedback*		*Make assessment decision and provide feedback*
		a	the decision is based on all the relevant performance and knowledge evidence available
a	success is confirmed when evidence is sufficient to infer competence over the range	b	when the combined evidence is sufficient to cover the range the performance criteria and the evidence specification, the candidate is informed of his/her achievement
		c	when evidence is insufficient, the candidate is given a clear explanation and appropriate advice
b	clear and constructive feedback is given following each assessment decision	d	feedback following the decision is clear, constructive, meets the candidate's needs and is appropriate to his/her level of confidence
c	candidate is encouraged to seek clarification and advice	e	the candidate is encouraged to seek clarification and advice
d	evidence and assessment decisions are recorded to meet verification requirements	f	evidence and assessment decisions are recorded to meet verification requirements
e f	records are legible and accurate records are passed on to the next state of the recording/certification process promptly	g	records are legible and accurate, are stored securely and are passed on to the next stage of the recording/certification process promptly
	Range *1. Records of:* assessment decisions; evidence *2. Candidate characteristics:* confident; lacking confidence; special needs		**Range** *1. Records of:* assessment decisions; evidence *2. Candidates:* experienced in presenting evidence; inexperienced in presenting evidence; candidates with special assessment requirements *3. Sufficiency of evidence:* sufficient to make the decision; insufficient to make the decision *4. Evidence derived from:* examination of products; observations of process; responses to questions

5 Guide to Unit D32: Assess Candidate Performance

This unit has four elements:

D321 – Agree and review a plan for assessing performance
D322 – Collect and judge performance evidence against criteria
D323 – Collect and judge knowledge evidence
D324 – Make assessment decision and provide feedback

D321: Agree and review a plan for assessing performance

Performance evidence is evidence that shows what someone can actually do. This can be demonstrated through what they do at work, what they produce at work or through special assignments, projects and, where necessary, simulations. Remembering what has been said about the different stages in the assessment process in Chapter 1, you will probably recognize D321 as the 'Planning stage' where you – the assessor – and the candidate are reaching an agreement about *what* will be assessed, *how* the assessment will be carried out and *when* it will take place. You will be ensuring that there is no confusion about the suitability of the evidence and that all the arrangements for the assessment have been organized and agreed.

D321a) *The opportunities identified are relevant to the elements to be assessed*

Explanation
An assessment opportunity is any occasion when the candidate is carrying out an activity which can be formally assessed. These opportunities for assessment will generally occur during their normal work, within a training programme or at a work placement. You, the assessor, need to make sure that the time(s) and place(s) arranged for the assessment actually offer the opportunity to assess the elements agreed between you and the candidate. For example, if you were intending to assess a candidate on how they worked in a team, it would be useless to arrange a time for assessment when they would be having no contact with other people. Similarly, if you were assessing a beauty therapy candidate on elements related to facial massage, it would be inappropriate to identify a time for assessment when a client wanted a leg-waxing treatment! Candidates for NVQs should be involved in identifying these opportunities and selecting which will be the most convenient and offer the possibility of covering a number of elements. GNVQ candidates should also be involved in assessment planning, although possibly assessment

opportunities in this case will often be defined through the assignments they are given.

Key points

■ *you can help the candidate relate what they are doing as part of their normal work to the units and elements to be assessed*

■ *you can help the candidate be aware of the possible opportunities for them to be assessed*

■ *you can involve the candidate in identifying appropriate opportunities when you could observe them and assess a number of elements or performance criteria.*

D321 b) Best use is made of naturally occurring evidence and related questioning

Explanation

The best way to judge if someone is competent at a particular task is to watch them at work and see how they perform. Your assessment should be based, as far as possible, on what the candidate is doing as a natural part of their work and on your observation of 'natural' performance. To give you an idea of the distinction between evidence that is 'naturally occurring' and evidence that is not, let us consider a situation where you are assessing a typist on certain elements related to typing a letter, eg, correct use of capitals, spacing and layout. All of these elements would 'naturally occur' as part of the process of typing a letter and could be assessed during an observation of the candidate typing a letter as part of his or her normal work. There might be a number of different contexts in which the candidate was working – in an office, in an open-learning workshop or in a classroom situation – but in each case it would be perfectly natural to type an entire letter as part of their normal duties. If you wished to check that a candidate was competent in these elements across a range of work contexts or using a range of different letter formats, then you would probably question them after the observation to make sure they were able to operate under differing conditions and that they knew the appropriate conventions. If the questioning did not provide you with enough evidence that the candidate was competent, then you would ask for some alternative evidence such as authenticated samples of letters typed on other occasions. If unsure about what alternative evidence would be acceptable, you would ask the advice of your internal verifier.

However, if your candidate needed to be assessed on layout and spacing in a stock order form and they did not do this as a normal part of their work, you may decide that the easiest way to assess these elements would be to set a short exercise on producing a stock order form covering the specific elements to be assessed. This would not be 'naturally occurring' evidence, but an artificial situation (a simulation) set up solely for the purpose of enabling the candidate to demonstrate a specific set of competences. In order that the candidate should still have the opportunity to achieve the NVQ, this alternative way of providing evidence would have to be made available.

Candidates on GNVQs will often be given projects so they can be assured that their evidence will cover all of most requirements of an element. So, for example, candidates in GNVQ in health and social care will be given a project on investigating one area of legislation in a health and social care context which will cover the requirements of an element on legislation and funding. These projects are still 'naturally occurring' as they are a part of the candidates' normal work in school or college. Core skills should occur as a natural part of this work and not as an additional 'bolt on' component.

The best use you, as an assessor, can make of naturally occurring evidence is to use it as a starting point for discussion with the candidate on what evidence could be used to prove competence, ie, begin with what is already there in what they are actually doing, rather than what needs more work to produce or design. It is useful to remember that, if organized properly, a considerable number of performance criteria can be evidenced through one observation.

Key points
- *you are aware of the different types of evidence that a candidate could provide*
- *you can distinguish between naturally and non-naturally occurring evidence*
- *you are aware of the cost implications of different types of evidence and assessment*
- *you are clear about the knowledge and understanding you need to assess in your area of work*
- *you know how to use different types of questions to find out what your candidate knows*
- *you can help the candidate decide how much can be evidenced through what they normally do as part of their work*
- *you are able to identify situations where a simulation would be the best way of evidencing.*

D 321 c) Opportunities are selected to minimise disruption to normal activity

Explanation
The key thing to remember here is that you are trying to assess candidate's *natural* performance and that anything which disrupts the candidate will affect their capacity to perform as they normally would. Hence if you, as the assessor, made yourself very obtrusive by being noisy, waving around a notebook or by positioning yourself somewhere that was unnecessarily obstructive, you could disturb the candidate's concentration and affect their ability to perform to their normal level of competence. Of course, in some

situations candidates will be used to being observed on a regular basis. For example, in a motor vehicle workshop supervisory staff will be moving around all the time checking on work being done. Similarly, in an open-learning workshop, candidates will be used to staff circulating and being available for consultation. In situations such as these, candidates are less likely to be disturbed than in a situation where candidates are not used to being observed, eg, a candidate being assessed as a trainer may never have had an observer with them in the training situation. GNVQs will often involve projects which are set in groups and assessed after being collected in. However, the assessments should be organized so that candidates who have handed in their evidence for assessment do not experience a major disruption to their timetable by being prevented from moving on to work for their next assessment. This can sometimes happen when tutors give extra time to candidates who have not kept to the time-scale identified in the assessment plan to submit their evidence, which means that everyone else is hanging around waiting for them to finish.

Key points
- *you have considered ways of preparing the candidate so that they will feel relatively at ease*
- *you have discussed the practical aspects of the assessment with the candidate and found out whether the candidate or other people in their work/training environment are likely to be disturbed by the assessment*
- *if you are observing, you have considered where you will position yourself and how you will conduct the assessment to cause the minimum disruption*
- *you have taken into account situations where you need to be very close to the candidate, eg, observing health and safety procedures, and ensured that you can assess in the most appropriate situation and can see clearly the task that is being performed*
- *you have taken the individual needs of the candidate into account (see Chapter 3).*

D321 d) Opportunities are selected which provide access to fair and reliable assessment

Explanation
A candidate who worked on a night shift, but was forced by their assessor to be assessed during the daytime without having had the chance to sleep, would not have been given access to fair assessment. Nor would the assessment give a reliable indication of how that person could perform in normal circumstances. Candidates at college, working towards a GNVQ in media, who were told that they would be assessed on producing a video, but unfortunately with only one video camera between 25 of them, would not have been given the best opportunity to demonstrate their abilities. Figure 5.1 on

These are some situations which could affect the candidate's access to assessment

Physical
If a candidate was in a wheelchair and the practical assessments were to take place on the first floor of a building with no wheelchair access

Chronological
If assessments always took place after 3.30 p.m., parents who had to collect children from school could be disadvantaged

Linguistic
If a candidate's mother tongue was not English, they could have difficulty understanding the assessment requirements

Social
If a candidate was lacking in confidence, they could be too nervous to submit themselves for assessment

Intellectual
If a candidate had learning difficulties, they could need much more support before they were ready for assessment

Resource-based
If the resources, eg, equipment needed for assessment, were not readily available, candidates would not have the opportunity to be assessed

Figure 5.1 *Examples of barriers to access to assessment*

barriers to access gives some examples of the difficulties which might be experienced by candidates.

Key points
- *you are aware of the problems candidates might have to access assessment*
- *you have explored the different types of opportunity that might be appropriate*
- *you have agreed the most appropriate way with the candidate.*

D321e) When simulations are proposed, accurate information and advice is sought about their validity and administration

Explanation
Although you are not expected to devise simulations yourself, you need to be able to find out what is available and how they need to be organized. In most cases the 'real thing' is obviously preferable, but there may be times when this is not possible – in situations or contingencies where a 'what if?'

question will not provide sufficient or valid evidence that the candidate can actually do something. This could occur when:

- someone needs to show that they can cope in a crisis or emergency situation, eg, first aid, dealing with fire equipment
- they do not have the opportunity to demonstrate a particular element as part of their normal work, but without it the cannot achieve the qualification
- carrying out a simulation rather than the real thing will save tremendously on time and cost.

For example, candidates for an NVQ in management needed to give an oral presentation to achieve the qualification. If the assessor had visited each of them individually, it would have taken a very long time. Instead, they were each given a brief that involved them giving an oral presentation to specifically-defined client groups, eg, to a group of trainees beginning work in their organization. The candidates delivered the presentations to each other during a one-day session, treating the audience in each case as if it were their chosen client group. The candidates were then involved in both peer and self-assessment of their performance.

When you, as the assessor, use simulations, you need to have a clear idea of the brief, what resources are required, what time it will take, what role(s) the participants will take and you need to be sure that it can replicate not just the activities but the pressures of a real-life situation. For example, if someone is giving mouth-to-mouth resuscitation, it does not bode well for the patient if they take ten minutes getting ready. If someone is carrying out an in-tray exercise in an office simulation, the simulation may need to allow for all the other interruptions and time pressures that office life provides. To ensure that simulations are being treated consistently, you should liaise with other assessors and the verifier.

Key points
- *you are aware of different types of simulation*
- *you know where to find ideas for simulations*
- *you know what to take into account when setting them up*
- *you know who to ask for help if necessary.*

D321 f) The proposed assessment plan is discussed and agreed with the candidate and others who may be affected

Explanation
The assessment plan should give a clear indication of *what* will be assessed, *how* it will be assessed and *when* it will be assessed. To emphasize that this is not just a one-way process, the candidate(s) needs to have a chance to discuss the plan, to ask any questions and to offer any appropriate suggestions or amendments before agreement on the planned assessment is reached.

You, as the assessor, also need to be sure that they do understand what is required. This is perhaps relatively easy when you have only one candidate, but if you are discussing an assessment plan with a group of candidates, what means do you use to ensure that they are all clear on the planned assessment? The assessment plan should always be recorded in written form, although there may be some occasions when it is amended just prior to assessment. For example, if you had arranged to assess a candidate working towards an NVQ in manufacturing textiles on using an industrial sewing machine and they realized that this would also provide an opportunity for being assessed on some health and safety elements, you could agree this verbally and record the agreement on the original assessment plan. The other people who could be affected by the planned assessment will vary according to your work situation, but they might include:

- supervisors in the workplace to ensure that they did not alter the candidates' work duties at the last minute
- other assessors who want you to confirm an assessment that they have made
- other tutors or trainers who need to coordinate their assessments with yours
- technical staff to make sure that the appropriate facilities were made available
- clients of the candidates to be informed that they may be involved in the assessment feedback
- colleagues of the candidates who might be affected by the presence of an assessor.

Key points
- *you have planned properly for the assessment, including the feedback session*
- *the elements and performance criteria to be assessed have been identified*
- *the time and place or occasion for assessment have been identified*
- *the assessment plan is recorded in writing*
- *the candidate(s) has had the opportunity to discuss the assessment plan, clarify any issues and agree with what is arranged*
- *you have ways of checking that the candidate(s) is clear on what is required*
- *your assessment plan shows how it relates to all the performance criteria.*

D321g) If there is disagreement with the proposed assessment plan, options open to the candidate are explained clearly and constructively

Explanation
In NVQs, the candidate should be involved closely in the development of the

assessment plan, which should reduce the possibility for disagreement. Where evidence is negotiable, if the candidate disagrees with what evidence has been suggested, you need to discuss whether another source of evidence will do just as well. If the timescale for assessment is not appropriate, can it be readjusted?

It is important that you are clear in your own mind about what is, or is not negotiable and the candidate should be made aware of this. For example, if the awarding body requires a written test, the candidate must complete this even though they are unwilling. The options here are basically 'Either do it or you cannot get the qualification'. However you would obviously take into account whether the candidate is objecting because they need encouragement or more guidance in order to provide this sort of evidence. It may be that you cannot resolve the difficulties yourself. You may suggest another assessor to the candidate or that they talk to the internal verifier. You may feel that it would help if they talked to other candidates who have been through the process.

Key points
- *the candidates have had the opportunity to discuss the assessment plans and clarify any issues*
- *you have checked that the candidates are clear on what is required*
- *you are clear on what is or is not negotiable*
- *you are willing to explore the negotiable options*
- *you deal with the candidates with tact and encouragement.*

D321h) The assessment plan specifies the target element(s)of competence, the types of evidence to be collected, the assessment methods, the timing of assessments and the arrangements for reviewing progress against the plan

See examples of assessment plans in Chapters 9 and 10.

D321i) Plans are reviewed and updated at agreed times to reflect the candidate's progress within the qualification

Explanation
One of the problems with working with candidates on an individual basis is the danger that they will feel isolated and possibly drift along without tangible targets. Although candidates for GNVQs taking place within an educational setting will have regular tutor contact and tutorial times arranged, candidates taking NVQs in the workplace will not have this kind of structure. However, it is important that there is the same possibility of monitoring progress and setting new targets. You, as the assessor, need to be aware of this and develop a system for keeping in contact. This might involve arranging monthly meetings, for example, or it might involve meeting when certain

targets have been achieved. The way you decide to do this will depend largely on the experience of the candidate and the amount of support and motivation they need from you.

Reviews should always be documented in some way and any revision of action plans recorded.

Key points
- *you set up a system for monitoring progress and setting targets*
- *you take into account the level of support a candidate might need*
- *you document the review.*

D322: Collect and judge performance evidence against criteria

Having dealt with the planning for assessment in D321, the next element relates to the actual process of assessing *performance* evidence. This should be differentiated from the assessment of *knowledge* evidence which will be covered in D323.

D322a) Advice and encouragement to collect evidence efficiently is appropriate to the candidate's needs

Explanation
Note that the responsibility for the identification and presentation of appropriate evidence is with the candidate and not with the assessor, although some candidates will need more help and advice than others. A mature individual, experienced in the NVQ or GNVQ approach, who has been well briefed on what sort of evidence is required, will probably start to organize the evidence fairly quickly. For example, a mature and confident candidate with considerable clerical experience is encouraged to consider what evidence she might be able to offer in order to claim competence in filing. She suggests that her present employer would be able to confirm the type and range of filing she does and it is agreed that she will get him to write a letter validating this claim. In this case, the candidate has only needed a little prompting and has been able to do the rest herself. However, a young, inexperienced candidate might need a lot more help and direction in identifying and compiling appropriate evidence. In a college of further education or a school, they might be given projects or assignments which are specifically designed to achieve a number of elements and performance criteria. Certainly in GNVQs this would be part of the school or college programme. All candidates when they begin will need advice about how to organize their paper-based evidence into an accessible format (see Chapter 10). In all circumstances, your candidates should aim to use strong evidence which will cover a number of performance criteria.

Key points
- you are aware of the benefits of candidates actively participating in the assessment process
- you help and encourage the candidate to identify evidence which might cover a number of performance criteria
- you ensure that the candidate is clear about the quality of the evidence required
- you provide opportunities for the candidate to suggest evidence
- you make sure the candidate knows how to organize themselves to collect and present evidence.

D322b) Access to assessment is appropriate to the candidate's needs

Explanation
The access referred to here is the access to assessment and the barriers to access could be, amongst others, physical, chronological, linguistic, social or related to intellectual capability (see the examples of barriers to access in Figure 5.1). What you, the assessor, must ensure is that no one who wishes to be assessed should be debarred from access to assessment, as long as they have the potential capability for the level indicated for assessment. Obviously, it would not be appropriate for a 16-year old welder to be assessed for NVQ level 5 in management. The barriers to assessment here would be unsuitability of level and occupational area over which you would have no control. However, that 16-year old welder should have a full opportunity of being assessed in welding at a realistic level, even if he has hearing difficulties or even if he can only work on a Tuesday and Saturday (look also at the explanation for D323c).

Key points
- you are aware of different barriers to access including special needs and lack of confidence
- you have made or would make arrangements to overcome these barriers
- you recognize that is the candidate's need for assessment rather than the assessor's priorities which should be considered first.

D322c) Only the performance criteria specified for the element of competence are used to judge the evidence

Explanation
The specified performance criteria are those already agreed by you and the candidate in the assessment plan where you identify the element(s) to be covered. This means that the candidates should only be assessed on the elements and performance criteria which have been agreed in the assessment plan. This avoids a situation which could be unfair to the candidate, eg,

assessing a trainer on how they use visual aids when you had only agreed to assess them on presenting information to learners. Remember that the intention of the standards is always to make the process of assessment *overt and understood*.

Key points
- *you only make judgements on pre-agreed performance criteria as stated in the assessment plan*
- *you ensure that the candidate is always clear on what is being assessed*
- *you only make alterations to the agreed assessment plan after discussion with the candidate*
- *you make sure that all performance criteria are covered.*

D322d) Evidence is judged accurately against all the relevant performance criteria

Explanation
The major question here is, 'How do you ensure that your assessment is accurate?'. There are various ways that your assessment could be *in*accurate. You might be unclear about what the elements and performance criteria actually mean, which would lead you to misinterpret what was actually needed to demonstrate competence. You might assess according to your own personal interpretation of the criteria without checking that your interpretation is in line with that of the other assessors and verifiers. You might place more emphasis on some criteria than others, or even miss some out, according to your own personal prejudices about what constitutes competent performance within the area you are assessing. You may have the impression that a candidate is very able and so fail to notice that, in fact, they are not performing to the standard required on a few of the elements. Think about whether these or other examples could apply in your own work situation and then consider how you ensure that your assessments are accurate.

Key points
- *you are aware of ways in which you might assess inaccurately*
- *you follow procedures and systems which ensure that you do assess accurately*
- *you are up-to-date with awarding body requirements*
- *you know who you should ask for help or clarification*
- *you are clear that all relevant performance criteria need to be demonstrated.*

D322e) The evidence is valid and can be attributed to the candidate

Explanation
Because performance evidence is generally generated through the observa-

tion of natural performance, you as the assessor will probably have actually seen the candidate do the work and questioned them personally to establish competence or achievement across the range. However, there might be some situations where this is less clear-cut. Obviously, using APL, the evidence has not been provided from your own observation and safeguards will have to be in place to ensure that it does refer to the candidate. One example of this would be a letter of validation from a previous employer. This should be on official headed notepaper or marked with the official stamp. Another situation where there might be problems about authenticity could be when you are assessing a product that has been presented as evidence. For example, if a candidate in catering showed you a cake they had prepared, you might ask them to describe how they had made it, what ingredients they used, the temperature they used while cooking – in fact, as many questions as you needed to feel sure that they knew what they were talking about. You still might not be satisfied, so you might ask to talk to their supervisor who could confirm that they had made it, or if that was not possible, to have a written witness statement from someone reliable.

Key points
- *you have checked out any evidence, such as product evidence or for APL that has not been observed by an accredited assessor by questioning, or asking for third-party confirmation*
- *evidence such as photographs are accompanied by the approved authentication.*

D322f) Any pre-set simulations and tests are administered correctly

Explanation
The simulations and tests referred to in this section are concerned with checking the skills and range covered in natural *performance*, whereas in D323 they are concerned with *knowledge* of the task or process. The difference between the two might best be explained by giving an example of two horticultural questions about the propagation of seedlings:

- a question related to performance would ask, 'How would you shield these seedlings from light?' and the method could be demonstrated if the equipment were available
- a question related to knowledge would ask, 'Why would you shield those seedlings from light?', which would explain why the process was being carried out.

The 'pre-set' simulations and tests in both these contexts mean any form of simulation or test which you have prepared or identified from a bank of suitable materials *in advance*, as opposed to, for example, questions that you might ask during the course of an assessment that you have not thought about beforehand (see Chapter 3 for general information on testing).

Pre-set tests can be prepared written tests or examinations, simulations which have been set up to test skills which cannot be demonstrated as part of normal work, or they can be a set of questions which you, the assessor, wish to have answered orally during an assessment interview, but which are written down for your own reference. Because these pre-set tests are part of a formal assessment process, there must be a consistency in the procedures with which they are administered to ensure that the assessment process is fair. Some aspects of administration to consider include these questions – if you are giving written or oral tests how are they organized; what kind of resources are needed; what kind of safeguards against cheating need to be applied? For example, in a written examination, desks will be arranged separately, examination papers will arrive in sealed envelopes and there will be strict instructions about what candidates can bring into the room. The procedures for pre-set tests should be followed by everyone involved in the assessment process and should be written down so that they can be followed by anyone involved in the administration.

Key points
- *you are aware of the correct administration procedures for different types of tests and simulations*
- *you follow the correct procedures when you administer oral and written tests or simulations*

D322g) The assessor is as unobtrusive as is practicable whilst observing the candidate

Explanation
You may find you can refer to your evidence for D321d) in covering this performance criterion. However, note the use of the word 'practicable' here. Remember that your main function when observing a candidate is to ensure that you are assessing accurately against the elements and performance criteria agreed in the assessment plan. This means that you may need to be very close to the candidate for particular operations, perhaps to see what the candidate is doing or to hear what they are saying to a client. In cases like this, you may well be obtrusive, but it is necessary in order to do your job as an assessor properly. However, you will obviously try your best to distract the candidate as little as possible and it is up to you to decide how to minimize the disruption (see Chapter 3 for notes on observation techniques).

Key points
- *you are aware of the benefits and problems of observation as a means of collecting assessment evidence*
- *you are aware of ways in which you might be obtrusive*
- *you have considered how to minimize the disruption.*

D322h) Evidence is judged fairly and reliably

It might be easier to clarify these terms in relation to your own situation if you considered ways that you felt might *not* be fair and reliable. For example, if you had a personal dislike for a candidate you might tend to be more critical about their performance than a candidate who you favoured. In another example, you might be in a hurry one day and rush through the assessment of one candidate, making a quick judgement on their competence rather than allowing a proper period of time to assess thoroughly. The next day, you might have plenty of time and spend a considerable period on the assessment of another candidate. And again, you might be assessing candidates for the same period of time but under very differing external conditions, eg, assessing for an NVQ in horticulture could involve assessing one candidate in perfect weather conditions and another candidate in driving rain. You could discriminate against candidates in a number of other ways. Candidates with school-age children might have problems if you insisted on assessing them late in the afternoon. Candidates whose first language was not English might have difficulties in producing an assignment for a GNVQ assessment and might need some extra language help initially. Your job as an assessor is to ensure that candidates would not be advantaged or disadvantaged because of these or other factors. Ask yourself the questions, 'What circumstances in my area of work might cause me to be unfair?', 'How do I compensate for them?' and, 'How do I really make sure that I am fair in my assessments?'

The reliability of your assessment is another vital factor. How can you really be sure that the candidate is competent and that what you have seen is not purely a 'one-off' phenomenon? In order to be competent, a candidate must be able to perform consistently to the same standard in a range of different situations. If a candidate is only assessed once, then how can you be sure that your assessment is a reliable indication of their ability to perform? In addition, how can you be sure that if another assessor assessed the same candidate that they would reach the same decision as you? (see Chapters 1 and 3).

Key points

■ *you know what the terms 'fair', 'unfair discrimination' and 'reliable' mean in relation to assessment*

■ *you are aware of where there might be a danger of your assessment being unfair or unreliable*

■ *you have considered how you can make sure that your assessment is fair and reliable*

■ *you understand and follow a set of procedures which ensure fair and reliable assessment*

■ *you take into account candidates' special assessment needs.*

D322i) Difficulties in judging evidence fairly and reliably are referred promptly to an appropriate authority

Explanation

There could be all sorts of reasons why you might have difficulties in making fair and reliable judgements. Your own personal standards of work might cause you to judge a candidate too harshly. You may be an expert in your vocational area, but got your own qualifications a number of years ago and are out of date in what you consider necessary. You may have difficulty with the level that you are assessing. For example, a teacher used to assessing 'A' levels and then being involved in assessing an assignment produced for a GNVQ level 2 might have difficulty determining whether the quality of work was appropriate to that level. In addition, you could find that the candidate disagrees with your judgement, or another assessor reaches a different conclusion. You may carry out a simulation and realize that some candidates are far more used to this type of activity than others, and have therefore performed far better. The best way to sort out these problems would be to refer to your internal verifier for advice and to refer back to the awarding body documentation for help. However you seek clarification, it is obviously important that you deal with the confusion as quickly as possible.

Key points

- *you have taken steps to ensure you understand the performance criteria*
- *you are clear on who you would refer to if you had any difficulties in interpretation*
- *you could give examples of areas where your judgement might not be fair or reliable*
- *you have considered different types of candidates with different levels of experience*
- *you have clarified any difficulties by consulting the appropriate documentation or individuals.*

D322j) The candidate is given clear and constructive feedback and advice following the judgement

Explanation

As an assessor, it is not enough just to tell the candidate whether they have been successful or not. Your role is also to let them know why you have made that decision. This is why the assessor should always set aside a proper time for discussion with the candidate so that both have time to talk over the result and the assessor is sure that the candidate fully understands the reasons for the assessment decision. Obviously, if the candidate has not yet achieved competence, then it is particularly important that they are given specific indications of where they need to improve in a constructive way that will motivate them for the next time they are assessed.

(See also 324d).

D323: Collect and judge knowledge evidence

From your observation of the candidate you, as the assessor, will be making a judgement on whether they have achieved the necessary elements as agreed in the assessment plan. However, you need to be sure that the conclusions you have drawn are accurate, as your assessment will be guaranteeing that the candidate can function in an occupational area to a national standard. To ensure that your inference of competent performance can be justified, you have to make sure that the candidate really knows what they are doing and that they will be competent across a range of different situations and contexts. The most straightforward way to find out is by questioning the candidate either orally or in writing. Even if oral testing is the only method used, the questions should be pre-set rather than being composed at the time. Some awarding bodies, eg, CITB have generated a bank of questions for each NVQ element and BTEC have generated end tests for GNVQ candidates, but in many cases, it is the responsibility of the assessor in consultation with other assessors and the internal verifier to compose their own 'bank' to be used. To devise these questions, you must become fully aware of the knowledge and understanding specifications for each element (see Chapter 3 on different types of questions).

D323a) Knowledge relevant to the element is identified accurately from the performance evidence

Explanation
When we look at someone carrying out an activity, we can often see that the individual knows how to do something under a particular set of circumstances. This may be sufficient for the knowledge requirements you are assessing. For example, in NVQ level 2 in retailing, the element involving recognition of hazardous goods and substances has a knowledge requirement that the candidate should know the location and use of protective clothing and equipment. When assessing, you might observe the candidate go to a store room or locker and put on some protective clothing. It would then be quite reasonable to infer that they had filled that particular knowledge requirement related to the element.

We can often infer a good deal about what someone knows by what they do or what they produce. For example, if we observe someone involved in child care instructing small children to wash their hands before eating, we can probably infer that the child care assistant knows at least one basic rule of hygiene. Similarly, if we are shown a completed press article produced by a journalist, we might infer that they know how to structure information and spell words correctly. However, we must be very careful in inferring how much someone knows from what we see them do. In the first example given, the child care assistant could just be copying what he has seen others do, without any knowledge of the reason why he is doing it, in which case he probably has no concept of the 'idea' of hygiene and hence would not be able to transfer this rule across to another situation. In the case of the journalist, we may be satisfied that she has produced the article herself, but has she used a dictionary to help her spell? Has she used a standard format to structure her article? In both examples, the key to assessing whether someone really knows something needs to be taken from the level of qualification. At lower levels, the definition of knowledge could just involve 'has information about' and the understanding required could be very limited. At higher levels, the definition of knowledge will probably include a deeper understanding of the knowledge aspects related to the element plus a broader ability to transfer and make connections between ideas and practice.

There are obviously difficulties in inferring knowledge from performance, particularly at higher levels. A notable exception to this is where the product evidence itself contains evidence of knowledge and understanding, as, for example, a GNVQ assignment which has involved both investigation and analysis, or a formal in-depth report on organizational training needs produced by a candidate involved in human resource development and presented as evidence for an NVQ in training and development. You, as the assessor, need to be familiar with what your candidates need to know and be clear about whether this can really be inferred through watching them perform or looking at what they have produced.

You need to consider whether more than one observation would give you the information you need, or perhaps whether a carefully constructed simulation might provide evidence. If you have any doubt, then you need to consider other ways to supplement this method.

Key points
- *you are aware of the knowledge and understanding needed for the relevant element(s)*
- *you have thought carefully about what knowledge evidence can realistically be demonstrated*
- *you are clear on what knowledge can be evidenced through seeing a candidate carry out an activity/ies or by examining what they have produced*
- *you are aware of some of the difficulties related to inferring knowledge from performance.*

D323b) Evidence of knowledge is collected when performance evidence does not cover fully the specified range or contingencies

Explanation
Even if you are assessing someone in the same organization as yourself, it may be quite difficult to cover the full range of situations and contingencies

purely through performance evidence. Because you, as the assessor, are making a *prediction* about whether the candidate will be able to perform consistently in a range of different contexts and situations, you need to feel confident that your judgement is an accurate reflection of their potential.

For example, a candidate for an NVQ in management has demonstrated competence in communicating a suggestion to subordinates, but you have not been able to observe that candidate communicating with someone in a position of higher authority. In order to judge that candidate's potential to communicate with people at all levels within an organization, you need to find out how she would communicate the same suggestion to her boss. It may be that you can arrange to see her do this if it is appropriate and does not take up much time, or maybe the candidate will put the suggestion in writing and you will be able to assess this. However, you may decide that the most straightforward way of finding out how she would deal with this situation is to ask her! The use of well-constructed and pertinent questions is an extremely useful method of exploring what candidates would do in a different situation. For example, would the candidate communicate the suggestion to subordinates in the office in the same way as she would communicate it to those on the 'shop floor'? You can also use questions to explore how the candidate would cope with certain contingencies, as in the possible situation where her subordinates refused to accept the suggestion or her boss ignored it.

Key points
- *you have considered the range of potential situations in which the candidate might be required to perform*
- *you have considered the different contingencies that may arise*
- *you have devised or selected questions that will provide the relevant information.*

D323c) Valid methods are used to collect knowledge evidence

Explanation
There may be a significant number of occasions where performance evidence cannot cover what needs to be known. For example, an NVQ in care has an element on maintaining the confidentiality of information. Part of the range involves the knowledge of relevant legislation such as the Data Protection Act and the Medical Records Act. It is highly unlikely this knowledge could be demonstrated by an observation of the candidate with a client. You need to identify in advance the underpinning knowledge that it might be difficult to evidence through performance and, where appropriate, involve the candidate in deciding how this might be evidenced. Some ways of providing evidence for this knowledge are:

- asking the candidate a number of knowledge-based questions about legislation
- giving the candidate a written test on legislation
- observing the candidate running a special training session on legislation
- getting the candidate to write an essay on relevant legislation
- finding evidence from past experience where knowledge of legislation was used directly.

When choosing the best way of providing evidence, it is important to ensure that the evidence demonstrates what it should be demonstrating. This sounds obvious, but too often assessors appear to be assessing someone's ability to write good English, rather than whether they have a good grasp of the knowledge required. Remembering the importance of removing barriers to access to assessment, you should always consider the most valid way for a candidate to demonstrate their knowledge. This should take into account their particular needs, for example, whether it would be fairer to test them in writing or orally. Someone who had worked for many years at a machine on a factory floor might not have had to do much writing. To test that person's knowledge by setting them a written test could be unfair (unless of course it was a requirement of the awarding body) and might not produce a reliable indication of what they really know. You should be clear in your own mind why the method chosen is a valid one and will provide the necessary evidence that the candidate is competent.

The questions you use should ensure that the range is covered and, if asked, you should be able to justify why you have used them. You should always bear in mind that in your assessments, you are predicting how someone will perform in future, ie their potential performance, and you should be able to justify your decision if necessary (cf the original standards – inferences of competent performance can be justified).

Apart from this, you also need to consider the time and cost involved in different types of evidence. Finding out what someone knows through an individual face-to-face interview is more time-consuming and costly than getting a group of candidates together for a written multiple-choice test. To check you are using these methods correctly, as usual, talk with your internal verifier and be familiar with the awarding body guidelines.

Key points
- *you are clear what knowledge evidence still needs to be provided*
- *you make sure that the evidence provides a genuine reflection of what the candidate knows*
- *you make sure that the evidence demonstrates what is required in the element(s)*
- *you do not discriminate against the candidate because of the methods used*
- *you check with your internal verifier if you need help or advice.*

D323d) When questions are used, they are clear and do not lead candidates

Explanation
If your assessment of the candidate's knowledge and understanding is to be accurate then you must ensure that they answer the questions without any help from you. Your role is to make sure that each question is specific, easy to understand and not phrased in such a way that an answer is suggested or a bias on the part of the assessor is indicated. For example, a question like, 'Don't you think you should have cleared the work area before you began the next job?', is hardly a question at all, but an indication that the assessor thinks that the candidate has done something wrong. You will find more examples of different types of questions in Chapter 3.

Key points
- *you know what types of questions can confuse or lead a candidate*
- *you can choose or devise questions which can elicit information without suggesting an answer*
- *you know how to devise and ask questions in ways which can encourage open answers from candidates.*

D323e) Access to assessment is appropriate to the candidate's needs

See 322b).

D323f) The knowledge evidence conforms with the content of the knowledge specification and is judged accurately against all the relevant performance criteria

Explanation

Some mention has already been made about the difficulties in assessing knowledge evidence (see Chapter 3). In order to be fair and reliable you must ensure that the knowledge you want the candidate to demonstrate is closely tied in to what is identified in the element and does not wander into the realms of 'what you think the candidate should know', eg, NVQ retailing has an element on unpacking stock and one knowledge requirement relates to the candidate's responsibilities under the Health and Safety at Work Act. The assessor needs to be clear that, in this instance, they are only assessing the candidate's knowledge of health and safety in relation to unpacking goods, including lifting, carrying and correct use of equipment.

Much of the time the knowledge and understanding will be linked to the range the candidate needs to demonstrate. It is important here that you keep referring back to the performance criteria to make sure that each criteria is met.

Key points
- *you are clear what knowledge needs to be tested*
- *you make sure that all performance criteria are covered in the range.*

D323g) Evidence is judged fairly and reliably

See 322h).

D323h) Difficulties in judging evidence fairly and reliably are referred promptly to an appropriate authority

See 322i).

D322i) The candidate is given clear and constructive feedback and advice following the judgement

See 322j).

D324: Make assessment decision and provide feedback

Having completed all the observation and questioning necessary to make an accurate assessment, you now move to the last stage in the assessment process – deciding whether the candidate really has met all the requirements of the performance criteria and range, letting them know of your decision, discussing the result and recording your decision in the appropriate way.

D324a) The decision is based on all the relevant performance and knowledge evidence available

Explanation
If the evidence that has been presented has been agreed and is valid, then there should be no redundant pieces of evidence floating around. However, it is important to remember the 'halo' and 'horns' effect mentioned in Chapter 3 and not allow evidence which proves competence or achievement in one area to affect your judgement in another area. For example, you may observe someone carrying out a series of repairs and feel that they are able to perform competently. When you start questioning them on what they know about other types of equipment that they may have to use as part of their job, you find they know very little. It would be tempting to let them get away with it. However, if you are making a judgement that employers nationally are to find reliable, all the evidence available does not suggest that they are fully competent. All evidence must be weighed up and allowed to contribute to your decision.

Key points
- *you do not make judgements based on a selective view of evidence*
- *you are prepared to decide that someone is not yet competent if some of the evidence suggests this.*

D324b) When the combined evidence is sufficient to cover the range, the performance criteria and the evidence specification, the candidate is informed of his/her achievement

Explanation
You make a positive decision about a candidate when you have enough information to convince you that they will be able to perform to the level of national standards across a range of different situations. This does not mean that you need enormous amounts of information, only that there is enough information of the right kind. Candidates for GNVQs who will hand in particular assignments will probably get them back with comments and information on what has been achieved.

However, it is surprisingly easy in practice to forget to tell the candidate specifically what performance criteria or aspects of the range they have achieved, particularly when assessing performance through observation. You may decide to confirm competence as the assessment progresses but you still need to summarize for the candidate the full extent of what they have achieved. This also helps when checking against assessment plans to determine what further action to take. The confirmation of success may be given verbally, but there will always be a formal recording procedure involved at some stage.

Key points
- *you have sufficient evidence to be sure that the candidate can perform competently in a range of different situations*
- *you set aside a time to inform the candidate of your assessment decision*
- *the candidate is made aware of the assessment decision as soon as possible.*

D324c) When evidence is insufficient, the candidate is given a clear explanation and appropriate advice

Explanation
Evidence might be insufficient because there is too little of it, it is not relevant, or it is not up to the required standard. This is the point where a candidate might feel demotivated. However, if you can give them a clear indication of why the evidence is not sufficient, so that the candidate can go away with very concrete information about how to improve its scope or quality, then you have given them something to build on.

Agreeing on a time where the additional evidence will be provided will also give them a tangible goal. You might also consider whether the planning for assessment and the guidance given to the candidate on the necessary evidence was adequate.

Key points
- *make sure you give detailed and specific information about why evidence is not sufficient*

■ *you give them encouragement and something to work towards.*

D324d) Feedback following the decision is clear, constructive, meets the candidate's needs and is appropriate to his/her level of confidence

Explanation
See D322j).

You should be considering the different ways in which you might give feedback, depending on the type of candidate. Some candidates will have a good deal of confidence and all they will need is specific information on what other evidence to produce. For other candidates, the feedback process is essential to motivate and move them forward. In each case, the feedback should be seen as development and not just an end in itself (Some hints on constructive feedback are given in Chapter 3).

Key points
■ *you understand what is meant by clear and constructive feedback*
■ *you have planned in advance how to give the feedback and how to record it*
■ *you can adapt your feedback to accommodate the needs of the confident and less-confident candidate.*

D324e) The candidate is encouraged to seek clarification and advice

Explanation
When you have given feedback to a candidate, are you sure that they understand it? Are you sure that they know what to do with it? You may need to consider how you ensure that candidates have a proper opportunity to discuss the assessments with you, both in circumstances where they receive oral feedback face-to-face and where they receive written feedback. What means do you use in these situations to encourage them to discuss the assessment with you? How far are they aware of the feedback process and the active part they should play in order to get the most out of what they are told? All these are vital questions. The answers are not straightforward, but are bound up in the relationship that you manage to establish with the candidate, even if you have had little or no previous contact with them.

Key points
■ *you are aware of ways of encouraging discussion*
■ *the candidate is aware of the importance of asking about anything they are unsure of or which confuses them.*

NAME: *A Bliss*   UNITS OR ELEMENTS: *123*
                                                        abc

DATE OF ASSESSMENT: *1/2/93*

<u>Lifting and Handling Heavy Goods</u>

You put the candidate at ease by having a short, informal chat and then leading them again through the pre-agreed plan. At all times, you were keen to encourage the candidate to ask questions for clarification about the process. I was pleased that you reinforced the fact that I was there to assess <u>you</u> *rather than* <u>them</u>*, and explained the options of where I could position myself with safety.*

You were meticulous in your observation and noting of the tasks performed. The interweaving of oral questions with tasks was done naturally, so that questions were asked at appropriate points in the exercise.

At no time did you ask leading questions.

Any resources were to hand.

The candidate was invited to give his own comments on his performance first. In this way, he was able to suggest one area where he had not met the criteria (trolley on an incline) and you led him to tell you what needed to be done. You went over the whole exercise, picking out tasks done particularly well, and the few areas where, although competent, there was room for improvement. The candidate was at ease throughout. You completed the feedback by mutually arranging a time later that day for the exercise to be repeated.

This was a simulation in the training workshop, due to the hazardous nature of the task. You confirmed that once deemed competent in the simulation, the candidate will have the opportunity to practise the task in the normal work environment.

I observed informal documentation being completed and saw completed log books and composite records of other candidates.

Action to be taken:

Arrange for portfolio check with adviser

Ensure <u>your</u> *explanation of this assessment includes the fact that the candidate was lacking in confidence and the special steps you took.*

Assessor: *J. Owen*   Date: *2/1/93*

Figure 5.2 *Feedback to candidate for assessor award*

D324f) Evidence and assessment decisions are recorded to meet verification requirements

Explanation
The verification requirements here will probably be for both internal and external verification. Many organizations have their own system of recording evidence provided, assessment decisions and candidate progress; relevant details are then transferred across to meet external awarding body requirements. Discussions are usually held with external verifiers to ensure that there is no unnecessary duplication of information.

Key points
- *you have completed all the necessary documentation related to assessments*
- *you understand the verification requirements for your organization*
- *you have safe and secure storage for your records.*

D324g) Records are legible and accurate, are stored securely and are passed on to the next stage of the recording/certification process promptly

Explanation
The importance of meticulous record-keeping cannot be over estimated in the assessment process. However, in order for the records to be useful, other people, including verifiers, other assessors, appropriate administrative personnel and the candidates themselves should be able to make sense of them. This means, if they are hand-written, that people should be able to decipher them and if mistakes are made in the recording that they should be altered clearly and signed to indicate the error has been corrected by the assessor and not altered without authority. There are a number of ways that you might check that your assessment records are accurate; for example, you may check them with the candidate's own records – in log books etc., you may keep an ongoing record of candidate progress and a summative record to keep the final results – cross-checking between the two. The essential question for you to consider is how you check that you have not omitted anything or made any mistakes in recording candidates' achievements. You need to pass on records promptly to ensure that you avoid hoarding documents on your shelf, desk or filing cabinet which would prevent other assessors, verifiers or any centralized recording system from getting the information on candidates' achievements.

Key points
- *you check all your entries for accuracy*
- *you check all your written documents can be read by those who need to have access to them*
- *there is a system in place to ensure rapid processing of results*
- *you inform all those concerned that assessments have taken place*
- *you are aware of the stages in the recording/certification process*
- *you organize yourself to pass on records as soon as practicable*
- *other people involved in the assessment process can confirm that you pass on records promptly*
- *you have safe and secure systems and storage for your records.*

	Original (Pre-Summer 1994)		Revised (Post-Summer 1994)
Unit D33	Assess candidate using diverse evidence		Assess candidate using differing sources of evidence
Element D331	*Determine sources of evidence to be used*		*Agree and review an assessment plan*
a	possible sources of evidence are clearly related to the elements to be assessed	a	possible opportunities for collecting evidence are identified and evaluated against their relevance to the element(s) to be assessed and their appropriateness to the candidate's needs
b	all feasible sources of relevant evidence are considered		
c	sources of evidence selected make cost-effective use of time and resources	b	evidence collection is planned to make effective use of time and resources
d	access to fair and reliable assessment is ensured	c	the opportunities selected provide access to fair and reliable assessment
e	assessment plans are discussed and agreed with the candidate and others who may be affected	d	the proposed assessment plan is discussed and agreed with the candidate and others who may be affected
		e	if there is disagreement with the proposed assessment plan, options open to the candidate are explained clearly and constructively
		f	the assessment plan specifies the target element(s), the opportunities for efficient evidence collection, the assessment methods, the timing of assessments and the arrangements for reviewing the plan
f	requirements to ensure quality of evidence are identified	g	requirements to assure the authenticity, reliability and sufficiency of evidence are identified
		h	plans are reviewed and updated at agreed times to reflect the candidate's progress within the qualification
	Range		**Range**
	1. Sources of evidence: natural performance; simulations; projects and assignments; questioning direct assessment, judgement of other assessors; candidate and peer reports; candidate prior experience		*1. Opportunities for collecting evidence from:* natural performance; simulations; projects and assignments; questioning; candidate and peer reports; candidate's prior achievement and learning
			2. Evidence used for: own judgements; judgements by other people
			3. Candidates: experienced in presenting evidence; inexperienced in presenting evidence; candidates with special assessment requirements

Element D332	**Original (Pre-Summer 1994)** *Collate and evaluate evidence*		**Revised (Post-Summer 1994)** *Judge evidence and provide feedback*
a	candidate is encouraged to identify and present relevant evidence	a	advice and encouragement to collect evidence efficiently is appropriate to the candidate's needs
		b	access to assessment is appropriate to the candidate's needs
d	the evidence can be reliably attributed to the candidate	c	the evidence is valid and can be attributed to the candidate
c	only the specified performance criteria are used in forming judgements	d	only the criteria specified for the element are used to judge the evidence
b	evidence is accurately judged against elements and performance criteria	e	evidence is judged accurately against all the relevant performance criteria
f	adequate safeguards are operated to ensure authenticity of evidence and currency of competence	f	when evidence of prior achievement/learning is used, checks are made that the candidate can currently achieve the relevant national standard
		g	evidence is judged fairly and reliably
e	inconsistencies in the evidence available are clarified and resolved	h	difficulties in authenticating and judging evidence are referred to the appropriate authority promptly
		i	when evidence is not to the national standard, the candidate is given a clear explanation and appropriate advice
		j	feedback following the decision is clear, constructive, meets the candidate's needs and is appropriate to his/her level of confidence
	Range *1. Sources of evidence:* natural performance; simulations; projects and assignments; questioning; direct assessment; judgement of other assessors; candidate and peer reports; candidate's prior experience		**Range** *1. Evidence derived from:* natural performance; simulations; projects and assignments; questioning; candidate and peer reports; candidate's prior achievement and learning *2. Evidence used for:* own judgements; judgements by other people *3. Candidates:* experienced in presenting evidence; inexperienced in presenting evidence; candidates with special assessment requirements

	Original (Pre-Summer 1994)		Revised (Post-Summer 1994)
Element D333	*Make assessment decision and provide feedback*		*Make assessment decision using differing sources of evidence and provide feedback*
d	assessment decision is based on all relevant evidence available	a	the decision is based on all relevant evidence available
		b	any inconsistencies in the evidence are clarified and resolved
a	success is confirmed when evidence is sufficient to infer competence over range	c	when the combined evidence is sufficient to cover the range, the performance criteria and the evidence specification, the candidate is informed of his/her achievement
g	further sources of evidence are identified when insufficient evidence is available to make a positive decision	d	when evidence is insufficient, the candidate is given a clear explanation and appropriate advice
b	clear, constructive feedback is given following each assessment decision	e	feedback following the decision is clear, constructive, meets the candidate's needs and is appropriate to his/her level of confidence
c	the candidate is encouraged to seek clarification and advice	f	the candidate is encouraged to seek clarification and advice
		g	evidence and assessment decisions are recorded to meet verification requirements
e	records are legible and accurate	h	records are legible and accurate, stored securely and passed to the next stage of recording/certification process promptly
f	records are passed to the next stage of the recording/certification process promptly		
	Range		**Range**
	1. Records of: assessment decisions; evidence		*1. Records of:* assessment decisions; evidence
	2. Candidate characteristics: confident; lacking confidence; special needs		*2. Candidates:* experienced in presenting evidence; inexperienced in presenting evidence; candidates with special assessment requirements
	3. Evidence: sufficient to make decision; insufficient to make decision		*3. Evidence:* sufficient to make decision; insufficient to make decision; own judgements; judgements made by other people
			4. Evidence derived from: natural performance; simulations; projects and assignments; questioning; candidate and peer reports; candidates' prior achievement and learning

6 Guide to Unit D33: Assess Candidate Using Differing Sources of Evidence

This unit has three elements:

D331 – Agree and review an assessment plan
D332 – Judge evidence and provide feedback
D333 – Make assessment decision using differing sources of evidence and provide feedback

D331: Agree and review an assessment plan

D331 is the planning stage for assessments using a variety of sources of evidence – not only natural performance, simulations, projects and assignments, questioning, using direct assessment by you, the assessor, but taking into account the judgement of other assessors, self-assessment by the candidate, peer assessments and also the prior experience of the candidate. You may wish to look at Chapter 9 which gives a list of different sources of evidence.

D331a) Possible opportunities for collecting evidence are identified and evaluated against their relevance to the element(s) to be assessed and their appropriateness to the candidate's needs

Explanation
The candidate should be involved in this planning process. With an NVQ, a good starting point is getting them to talk through what they do at present and, from there, making suggestions about what could be used, remembering that performance evidence should always form a substantial part. With GNVQs, assignments and other activities will have been designed with specific elements in mind. As with all elements in the awards, the evidence offered must provide specific proof that the candidate is competent in that area. This is to avoid, for example, the 'shopping trolley' approach where the candidate brings along a pile of evidence in the hope that something they have brought will prove them competent.

Key points
- *you have explored the various opportunities for collecting evidence*
- *you have agreed on elements to be assessed*
- *you have discussed and agreed an assessment plan relevant to the candidate and their needs*
- *you have discussed possible sources of evidence with the candidate*

- *you have made sure that the candidate is clear about what they have to prove*
- *you have advised the candidate that they should clearly identify the competences claimed.*

D331b) Evidence collection is planned to make effective use of time and resources

Explanation
If the assessment process is organized effectively you and the candidate should have discussed what evidence will be appropriate and relevant to the elements agreed in the assessment plan. You will also have discussed which evidence will be most feasible, taking into account how much time it will take and how expensive it will be. For example, direct observation may take a considerable amount of time and would be costly in terms of the assessor's time, but a large number of elements could be covered in one well-planned observation visit. A simulation set up in order to assess one candidate may well be too costly, but if it were planned so that a number of candidates could be assessed at the same time it could actually turn out to be cheaper than other methods. The resources mentioned here could be people or physical resources such as room or workshop space, equipment and materials. It is important to remember that one piece of evidence can cover a number of performance criteria.

Key points
- *you are aware of the implications of the term 'cost-effective'*
- *you have considered the advantages and disadvantages of different types of evidence in terms of time and resources*
- *you have considered how a number of performance criteria can be covered by the same evidence*
- *you are clear on awarding body requirements.*

D331c) The opportunities selected provide access to fair and reliable assessment

Explanation
See D321d) but note that for this element you have to demonstrate how you ensure this access for different types of evidence. For example, you could use candidate self-assessment as part of the evidence. A candidate diary would be a useful means of doing this for those used to writing more at length, but some candidates would find it very difficult. A specially-designed proforma would be simpler to use, allow you to be more objective, but would not give the opportunity to provide evidence of deeper knowledge and understanding.

Key points
- *you have made sure that the opportunities do not disadvantage the candidate*

- *you are clear about the possible barriers created by certain types of evidence.*

D331d) The proposed assessment plan is discussed and agreed with the candidate and others who may be affected

See D321f).

D331e) If there is disagreement with the proposed assessment plan, options open to the candidate are explained clearly and constructively

See D321g).

D331f) The assessment plan specifies the target element(s), the opportunities for efficient evidence collection, the assessment methods, the timing of assessments and the arrangements for reviewing the plan

See examples of assessment plans in Chapters 9 and 10.

D331g) Requirements to assure the authenticity, reliability and sufficiency of evidence are identified

Explanation

In your assessment planning, the candidate should have been given clear information and advice about the evidence needed. You will have discussed the importance of not including unsubstantiated documents and what signatures or official stamps are needed to authenticate these (see Chapter 9). You should have emphasized that it is not the amount, but the quality of evidence that is needed and established some indicators of how much is actually required eg, three typed letters using a particular format: an assignment of approximately 800 words. You should also have discussed with other assessors and with the internal verifier what you understand by good quality evidence, so that there is consistency in the information being given to candidates.

Any assessment system where candidates can bring evidence from their previous experience is obviously open to abuse. An unscrupulous candidate could persuade friends to write testimonials or could use someone else's work, whether written or manufactured and pass it off as their own. Even testimonials from line managers could sometimes be suspect in that it is sometimes difficult to refuse a colleague (even an incompetent colleague) a witness statement without giving offence. You, the assessor, have to be sure that the evidence being presented is genuine and, if you have any suspicions, need mechanisms by which you can establish its authenticity. For example, assessment of the core skill 'communication' might be problematic if a candidate produced a formal report which they claimed had been written by them and you wanted to be sure this really was so. There are a number of ways you might establish that it really was the candidate's own work:

- you might ask them a number of questions about the work
- you might ask for a signed statement from the person who had assessed the report
- you might ask the candidate to write a short piece while you observe and compare it with the report for any obvious inconsistencies in vocabulary or style.

In every case there should be safeguards and procedures in place to ensure that you are guided in what is acceptable and you can ask for advice if in doubt.

Key points
- *you understand the terms 'authentic', 'reliable' and 'sufficient'*
- *you have agreed these with other assessors and the internal verifier*
- *you can apply these to your own area of work*
- *you are aware of the guidelines for evidence requirements of the relevant awarding body*
- *you follow the necessary procedures to ensure authenticity and reliability*
- *you are sure that the candidate is also clear on what is needed.*

D331h) Plans are reviewed and updated at agreed times to reflect the candidate's progress within the qualification

See D321i).

D332: Judge evidence and provide feedback

This is the stage where the different sources of evidence are gathered together and the assessor judges whether the evidence meets all the necessary requirements.

D332a) Advice and encouragement to collect evidence efficiently is appropriate to the candidate's needs

See D322a).

D332b) Access to assessment is appropriate to the candidate's needs

See D322b).

D332c) The evidence is valid and can be attributed to the candidate

Explanation
See D322e) which deals with performance evidence. However, as you may not have observed the candidate producing the evidence, you need to show how you ensure that they really have. You will probably use various safeguards to ensure that it is authentic, for instance, in a written test, you will

make sure that the candidate has not copied from anyone else. One particular problem occurs when the candidate is working as part of a group. This is where self-assessment by the candidate and peer assessment by the rest of the group can confirm the candidate's claim and prove its authenticity.

Key points
- *you make sure the evidence is produced by the candidate*
- *you use a number of different methods, including self- and peer assessment where appropriate, to confirm the candidate's claim.*

D332d) Only the criteria specified for the element are used to judge the evidence

See D322c) but note here that you are forming judgements based on a *variety* of evidence rather than just assessing performance. However, in either case, the performance criteria should have been identified in the assessment plan.

D332e) Evidence is judged accurately against all the relevant performance criteria

Explanation
See D322d). However, here you will have to give more detail about how you ensure that the different types of evidence other than purely performance evidence are assessed accurately. You could do this by giving a few examples of how you deal with different types of evidence, eg, an assessor of GNVQs might have to assess candidate diaries or group projects; an assessor of NVQs might have to deal with anything from client record cards to large-scale company reports presented as evidence.

Key points
- *you are clear what performance criteria the evidence is addressing*
- *you have consistent systems for assessing different types of evidence agreed with other assessors and your internal verifier.*

D332f) When evidence of prior achievement/learning is used, checks are made that the candidate can currently achieve the relevant national standard

Explanation
When candidates wish to use evidence from APL, an issue to consider is how up-to-date the evidence of competence actually is. Someone producing a computing qualification dating from the late 1970s will not be providing evidence of *current* competence in modern computer technology, whereas a qualification that is only one year old may well be acceptable. Currency of competence is obviously particularly important in areas where machines or equipment are in use; however, there may be other areas, for example, the care sector, where a qualification obtained a number of years ago may still be judged appropriate and sufficient.

If in any doubt, the most straightforward way of checking is through watching them carry out the relevant process or activity, eg, ask to see the candidate carry out a number of different functions using a modern computer. If this is time-consuming or expensive, then letters of validation or witness testimonies that they are currently competent might be sufficient.

Key points
- *you are familiar with the current requirements in your occupational area*
- *you have thought about where knowledge or skills might have become out of date*
- *you have the means of checking if they are currently competent if necessary.*

D332g) Evidence is judged fairly and reliably

See D322h).

D332h) Difficulties in authenticating and judging evidence are referred to the appropriate authority promptly

See D322i). If a candidate produces evidence that may not be authentic, or where there is doubt, you would ask your internal verifier for their opinion.

D332i) When evidence is not to the national standard, the candidate is given a clear explanation and appropriate advice

See D324c).

D332j) Feedback following the decision is clear, constructive, meets the candidate's needs, and is appropriate to his/her level of confidence

See D322j) and D324d).

D333: Make assessment decision using differing sources of evidence and provide feedback

Having considered all the evidence presented, this is the point where you make your decision and discuss it with the candidate.

D333a) The decision is based on all relevant evidence available

See D324a).

D333b) Any inconsistencies in the evidence are clarified and resolved

Explanation
As you are making a judgement of someone's competence based on various

sources of evidence, there may well be some occasions where the level of competence suggested by one piece of evidence is not supported by other evidence. For example, you may have a written testimonial from a previous employer, stating that the candidate followed health and safety procedures, but the first-line assessor's report states that this was not obvious during a workplace observation. In this case, you would give them feedback that they had not met this requirement and, that during the next observation, this competence would need to be reassessed. In order to be sure, you would probably question them closely about their understanding of health and safety procedures and look for some kind of third party evidence as well, for example from their supervisor at work. In another example, a candidate working towards a GNVQ in business administration is being assessed by a number of different assessors. She appears to be having little difficulty in achieving elements related to filing, but a great deal of difficulty with elements related to stock-keeping. Here, you would probably ask yourself if the problem is with the candidate, or with a lack of consistency among assessors. If it is the candidate, are you sure that she can deal with numbers adequately or is this proving a barrier to achievement? To check this you might see how she is doing on her core skills *'Application of Number'*. If her numerical ability is adequate, does she have any problems with the tutor who is assessing her in stock-keeping? If she does not have any problems with the tutor, and no particular hatred of this area of work, you may want to look more closely at the level of consistency among assessors, eg, are some assessing more rigorously than others? Clarification will probably come by talking to the candidate, to other assessors and by asking for advice from the internal verifier.

Key points
- *you are aware of ways in which evidence can be inconsistent*
- *you are aware of the procedures to follow if you discover inconsistencies in evidence.*

D333c) When the combined evidence is sufficient to cover the range, the performance criteria and the evidence specification, the candidate is informed of his/her achievement

Explanation
In D33, you have to deal with a number of different sources of evidence and your decision needs to be based on everything submitted that is relevant, ie, that relates specifically to the elements identified in the assessment plan.

Your role is also to ensure that the candidate knows if the evidence they have presented meets the required standard.

Key points
- *you are sure you have taken every piece of relevant evidence into account*

■   *you check that all aspects of the element are covered.*

D334d) When evidence is insufficient, the candidate is given a clear explanation and appropriate advice

Explanation

There may be situations where you are not able to make a decision or not prepared to judge someone competent on the evidence available. This could occur when the candidate has not provided evidence of sufficient quality. For example, the candidate has brought you a witness statement written by a line manager, but it is so general that it does not back up their claim against specific elements. You might have to ask them to get another, more specific statement, or you might decide that you will arrange to observe them at work instead. Another situation could be that although a candidate has produced enough evidence against the performance criteria, they have not produced enough against the range. In this case, the assessor will discuss what else the candidate needs to produce. Yet another example could be where a candidate for a GNVQ has produced an assignment, but it is very short and sketchily done. The assessor in this case might tell the candidate that they need to go away and produce a longer and more detailed piece of work or that they need to produce an additional piece of work to compensate. Whatever the problem is, the candidate should be left with a clear idea of what they need to do to achieve sufficient evidence.

Key points

■   *you are clear what will be sufficient evidence*
■   *you make sure that the candidate knows what else is needed*
■   *you can offer candidates advice in a helpful way that does not exclude their right to make choices about what they wish to do.*

D333e) Feedback following the decision is clear, constructive, meets the candidate's needs and is appropriate to his/her level level of confidence

See D324d).

D333f) The candidate is encouraged to seek clarification and advice

See D324e).

D333g) Evidence and assessment decisions are recorded to meet verification requirements

See D324f).

D333h) Records are legible and accurate, stored securely and passed to the next stage of the recording/certification process promptly

See D324g).

	Original (Pre-Summer 1994)		Revised (Post-Summer 1994)
Unit D34	**Coordinate the assessment process**		**Internally verify the assessment process**
Element D341	*Provide advice and support to assessors*		*Advise and support assessors*
a	procedures are in place to ensure assessors possess necessary documents, records and guidelines	a	assessors are provided with full, up-to-date awarding body documentation, records and guidelines
b	training needs of assessors are identified and provision is made	b	assessors are given accurate advice and support to enable them to identify and meet their training and development needs
c	advice to assessors on additional evidence is prompt and in line with awarding body policy	c	accurate advice is provided about the appropriate and efficient use of different types of evidence
d	assessors are assisted with arrangements for special needs candidates	d	assessors are assisted with arrangements for candidates with special assessment requirements
e	assessors' duties are clearly allocated	e	allocations of assessor responsibilites are clear and match the needs of candidates and assessors
		f	accurate up to date advice and relevant support is provided to achieve consistency in assessments
	Range		**Range**
	Assessors: novice – experienced		*1. Assessors:* experienced; inexperienced
	Advice: provision of information; interpretation of guidelines/policy; responding to requests; anticipating needs		*2. Advice:* responses to assessors' requests; advice that anticipates assessors' needs; factual information; interpretation of guidelines/policy
			3. Assessor support: direct support; indirect support
			4. Evidence derived from: natural performance; simulations; projects and assignments; questioning; candidate and peer reports; candidate's prior achievement and learning
			5. Consistency in assessments one assessor over time; different assessors judging the same element(s)

	Original (Pre-Summer 1994)		Revised (Post-Summer 1994)
Element D342	*Maintain and submit assessment documentation*		*Maintain and monitor arramgements for processing assessment information*
b	submissions for award of certificates fully meet awarding body requirements	a	arrangements for monitoring candidate records and processing information meet awarding body requirements and are sufficient to assure quality
a	candidate records are complete, legible and accurate	b	candidate records are complete, legible and accurate
		c	candidate records provide accurate and up-to-date information on monitoring candidate progress within the qualification and the judgements and assessment decisions made
c	security and confidentiality are maintained	d	information is stored securely and disclosed only to those who have a right to it
	Range		**Range**
	Certificates: certificate of unit credit; full qualification		*1. Information processes:* for recording candidate information; for making submissions for the award of certificates

	Original (Pre-Summer 1994)		Revised (Post-Summer 1994)
Element D343	*Undertake internal verification*		*Verify assessment practice*
a	procedures are in place to ensure that assessors meet awarding body criteria for acting as an assessor	a	the eligibility of individuals to practise as assessors is checked against awarding body criteria
b	assessment practice is monitored and constructive feedback is provided	b	assessment practice and quality assurance arrangements are monitored in an appropriate proportion of instances to check that they meet awarding body requirements
		c	assessors are given clear and constructive feedback
c	assessments made conform to national standards	d	judgements of evidence and assessment decisions are sampled regularly against the national standards to check their fairness and accuracy
d	documentation is complete and up-to-date	e	documentation is complete, accurate and up-to-date
		f	decision makers are given clear explanations of the need for improvements in assessment practice
e	disputes and appeals are referred to the appropriate authority	g	disputes and appeals are referred to the appropriate authority
f	recommendations for external action to maintain quality of assessment are accurately communicated to external verifier	h	recommendations for awarding body action to maintain the quality of assessment are presented clearly and promptly to the external verifier
	Range *Sources of evidence:* natural performance; simulations; projects and assignments; questioning; direct assessment; judgement of other assessors; candidate and peer reports; candidates prior experience *Assessor support:* establishing assessor networks; training; briefing/advising/coaching		**Range** *1. Assessment practices:* awarding body requirements for evidence collection, assessment and internal verification; provision of access to fair and reliable assessment; production and maintenance of records; timely processing of assessment decisions *2. Quality assurance arrangements for:* authenticity; reliability; sufficiency; consistency *3. Recommendations relating to:* assessment methods; national standards

7 Guide to Unit D34: Internally Verify the Assessment Process

This unit is designed for those who undertake the role of internal verifier for a centre. The internal verifier candidate will also be expected to be competent in assessing using a wide range of sources of evidence, and will normally have already obtained, or be working towards, D33 and D32. There are three elements to D34:

D341 – Advise and support assessors
D342 – Maintain and monitor arrangements for processing assessment information
D343 – Verify assessment practice

D341: Advise and support assessors

The major role of an internal verifier is to be responsible for one or more assessors, depending on the size of the organization, offering them support and guidance on how best to organize their assessment role.

D341a) Assessors are provided with full, up-to-date awarding body documentation, records and guidelines

Explanation
There should be a *working* system, understood and used by all parties involved (which may include support staff if they are involved in distributing materials), that enables assessors to have all the awarding body documentation, records and guidelines that they need. There should be a clear procedure for receipt and distribution of materials and information.

The internal verifier needs to be sure that the system is actually working in practice. Documents will include not only the forms used by assessors in assessment practice, such as copies of the standards, observation checklists and certification sheets, but also information and guidance letters, publications and publication lists produced to assist assessors. Copies of NCVQ materials such as *NVQ Monitor* and lists of telephone numbers and addresses of awarding bodies may also be useful. As an internal verifier or internal verifier candidate, it can be helpful if you know the names and telephone extension of key people at the awarding body headquarters (as well as the external verifier) who can assist with queries or information.

The internal verifier must ensure that assessors understand and have either copies of, or access to, copies of relevant documentation. It would be useful to have a circulation list which ensures, through signatures, that people have received information. Regular meetings with assessors, formal or informal, are likely to generate discussion on national standards, quality assurance and the need for information.

Key points
- *you need to have a working system to keep a check on whether assessors have received or borrowed materials from you*
- *there must be evaluation of arrangements to check they are working effectively*
- *all materials need to be up-to-date.*

D341b) Assessors are given accurate advice and support to enable them to identify and meet their training and development needs

Explanation
The information received by assessors from awarding bodies and NCVQ, together with their own assessment practice, will prompt questions or requests for clarification from you as internal verifier. You need to ensure that advice is accurate – liaison with the external verifier will help, plus contact with awarding bodies, literature, and attendance at training events, where possible. All awarding bodies give guidelines on what they expect for assessment purposes and how they expect their assessments to be monitored. Awarding bodies require most assessors to be accredited by achieving units D32 and D33. Although this may well involve the training of staff towards this accreditation, it is not necessary for the internal verifier to do the training unless they are the most appropriate person. Your task is to see that the training needs can be identified and met, and to ensure that the assessor is able to take advantage of whatever provision is made, so that they can improve in practice, knowledge or understanding.

Key points
- *all assessors, whether new or experienced, need to regularly identify their training needs*
- *assessors should be helped to identify training needs and to meet them*
- *it should be simple for assessors to express their needs, as well as be helped to identify them*
- *there should be evidence of providing accurate support and advice related to training needs when necessary.*

D341c) Accurate advice is provided about the appropriate and efficient use of different types of evidence

Explanation
If you need to check that you are giving the correct advice, you will probably use your external verifier or a contact at the awarding body's head office. You will also know other internal verifiers who can double-check your interpretations.

Candidates' particular circumstances, both personal and work-related, will be likely to influence the type of evidence they present. The internal verifier can help to clarify doubts over such things as a portfolio which relies heavily on a particular type of evidence such as oral or APL. You will need to know how to interpret guidelines relating to items such as the amount of simulated and natural performance evidence permissible in particular circumstances. The range for this element lists the different types of evidence. See also chapter 9.

Key points
- *you should keep records of advice about different types of evidence that you have given to assessors*
- *you should be able to demonstrate the ways in which you are informed of awarding body policy*
- *records of advice should be dated, as should all requests to you, and key assessment activities.*

D341d) Assessors are assisted with arrangements for candidates with special assessment requirements

Explanation
Candidates will have a wide diversity of learning aptitude and life experience. They may need help from assessors in order for fair assessment to take place. A common form of assistance would be to liaise with support workers where a candidate has a visual or hearing impairment, or to arrange for an interpreter to be present should a candidate not be fluent in English. Other arrangements might consist of providing suitable accommodation for assessments to take place, providing staff cover to enable a candidate to be assessed in a quiet, stress-minimized environment, or to clarify with the external verifier procedures to be used in particular organizations, such as a young offender's institution. Night-shift workers or part-timers may need to make more use of video recordings of assessments. It might be necessary for internal verifiers to offer support by, for example, negotiating time off in lieu for assessors who have adapted their normal hours of work to accommodate an assessment, for example, on an evening or a Saturday, or to help sort our childcare arrangements. Arrangements for childcare may need to be considered for *all* of the parties involved in assessment.

The internal verifier will often be instrumental in helping to determine whether the proposed style of assessment is the most appropriate. A common example might be where a candidate, good at their vocational area, feels unhappy about producing a heavily paper-based portfolio, and requests oral assessment and observation with the minimum of written explanation. This might be harder on the assessor, but would be a lot fairer system for the candidate. The internal verifier could assist by giving direct support through observing the assessment, enabling the assessor to avoid having to write a lot of comment and concentrate more on the assessment process.

Key points
- *keep records of offers of and requests for support, together with action taken, relating to candidates with special assessment requirements*
- *be aware of possible problems for which assessors might need to make special arrangements, so that you can pre-empt delays in the assessment process*
- *ensure that candidates are able to access assessment fairly.*

D341e) Allocations of assessor responsibilities are clear and match the needs of candidates and assessors

Explanation
It is your job, as internal verifier, to ensure that duties are clear and unambiguous, and that assessors know what is expected of them. There will probably be lists of candidates, with assessor allocations, together with a written list of duties and procedures to be followed by assessors. It is likely that arrangements will be negotiated with assessors to ensure 'best match' of needs. The needs could include physical arrangements, such as time and place of assessments or the need to be assessed by someone with particular specialism.

Key points
- *ensure all assessors know what is expected of them*
- *negotiate duties where possible*
- *ensure that assessors are clear with whom they are working, and are aware of particular candidate needs.*

D341f) Accurate, up to date advice and relevant support is provided to achieve consistency in assessments

Explanation
Assessments can become inconsistent because a) there are a number of assessors who are interpreting advice in different ways; b) because an assessor is unsure about evidence presented by different candidates, particularly if they are operating in very different environments, and may 'give the benefit of the doubt' or, conversely, ask a candidate to provide extra evidence when it is not needed; or c) because a centre is isolated from other centres, or has inadequate support from an external verifier, leading to the possibility that their assessments may in time vary markedly from those of other centres. The internal verifier needs to be able to liaise with relevant persons *outside* the centre in order to discuss interpretations in assessment, as well as to be in regular contact with assessors to prevent inconsistencies and to resolve those which do inadvertently happen. If several assessors can meet together, exercises where the same evidence is assessed by the group can help to identify areas where different views may lead to inconsistency.

It is extremely important that internal verifiers keep up to date with national and regional advice to ensure the quality of the assessment practice.

Key points
- *identify likely instances of inconsistency*
- *keep abreast of awarding body views on interpretation of evidence*
- *arrange for assessments to be compared*
- *ensure communication regarding interpretation between all relevant parties.*

D342: Maintain and monitor arrangements for processing assessment information

It is the role of the internal verifier (often called the 'centre-named contact') to be responsible for the arrangements for, and monitoring of, the completion, submission and storage of all records connected with the assessment process. These records should be monitored regularly. There should be clear guidelines relating to the accessibility of candidate records, and the provision of suitable secure accommodation or furniture where records relating to assessment can be kept.

D342a) Arrangements for monitoring candidate records and processing information meet awarding body requirements and are sufficient to assure quality

Explanation
How often this is done per assessor will, of course, be dependent on the resources at the centres disposal. NCVQ are extremely concerned that quality assurance procedures can be seen to be working in practice. It is your job as internal verifier to ensure that you know how assessments are progressing within your organization. You should have a system of keeping in touch with what assessors are doing, whether candidates are being given sound guidance and whether records are being kept up to date.

The NVQ/SVQ/GNVQ/GSVQ systems allow for candidates to offer themselves for individual unit credit, as well as full qualification assessment. You should be fully aware of the procedures operated by the awarding bodies with which your centre is registered and be able to prove that your submissions fully comply. There will need to be evidence in the candidate's file of submitting both for unit and for full certification and you should have evidence of external verification, as well as copies of the documentation sent to the awarding body. This documentation will consist of at least a registration form and certification forms. Other documentation which you and the external verifier need to see are candidates' records of achievement, summaries of evidence, action and assessment plans, notes of advice and feedback, storyboards and evidence checklists. The correct completion of these will enable you to prepare accurate submissions for certification. You will probably need some lists to keep track of submission for certification especially if there are large numbers of candidates, for example:

Candidate	Reg. No/dob	Adviser	Assessor	EV
I Briggs	12345 8.8.64	C Jones	J Russell	M Griffin
A Akbar	67890 26.4.48	K Needham	C Jones	M Griffin

Key points
- *you need to be clear what quality assurance procedures are required by the awarding body*
- *you need to have a workable system of keeping a check on how both assessors and candidates are progressing*
- *check all aspects for completed submission material: signatures, candidate names, dates, award references*
- *random check candidate submissions against internal documentation and records.*

D342b) Candidate records are complete, legible, and accurate

Explanation
In practice, it is the assessors who will complete most of the documentation relating to candidates. The internal verifier needs to monitor the work of all assessors, regularly checking that *all* documentation, for example signatures and dates in log books, weekly reviews and test results, correspond with the final or cumulative records submitted for verification. It is only by being rigorous at this stage that accusations of malpractice can be refuted. You should be able to track a candidate's progress from start to finish. The original centre submissions should show the spread of documentation to be completed; centre-devised documentation needs to be compatible with the NVQ or awarding body documentation. You will need to check that candidates possess and are using the right documentation. In our experience, some workplace assessors can adopt a cursory approach to the marking of and commenting upon candidates' work relating to the achievement of tasks or to the giving of constructive feedback. It is therefore understandable that criticisms have arisen around the thorough testing of knowledge and understanding, which is an *integral* part of assessing natural performance. You should be satisfied that there are valid reasons for the omission of any part of the recording process for the candidates whose work has been checked, or for the alteration of any recording. It should be possible to check authenticity of signatures. One particular problem is the use of rubber stamps for signatures, as there would obviously be a temptation to forgery if they fell into the wrong hands.

Key points
- *keep spot checks rigorous to ensure quality standards are maintained*

- *support assessors by providing helpful materials, eg, NCR (no carbon required) sheets for assessments*
- *prepare samples of completed documentation to help assessors who are having difficulties.*

D342c) Candidate records provide accurate and up-to-date information on monitoring candidate progress within the qualification and the judgements and assessment decisions made

Explanation
The records kept on candidates should enable you to check the speed of progress (dates), whether there is negotiation and agreement between candidate and assessor (signatures), and assessment decisions (records and feedback with action plans). You will probably carry out spot checks on records (see 342b).

Key points
- *you know where candidate records are kept*
- *you keep in touch with the assessors and ensure that they know they will be monitored.*

342d) Information is stored securely and disclosed only to those who have a right to it

Explanation
The organization for whom you act as internal verifier needs a well-organized system to deal with assessment and certification. This may include computerized records and safe keeping for copies of all documents sent to and received from the awarding bodies. It is important that candidates are assured of confidentiality in dealing with their records; birth dates and personal information can be sensitive areas; some candidates may wish to keep quiet about the speed with which they are progressing through the system, or indeed, take qualifications without the knowledge of others. It is important that they know who will be allowed access to their personal confidential information, eg reviews, and records for certification. All assessors should have the space to keep records securely, eg, in a locked room or, preferably, locked filing cabinet or cupboard.

We have known problems arise where, for example, assessors have used candidates' work for moderation purposes, without first seeking their permission, or where work has been left on desks and has been looked at by other staff or candidates, again without permission.

Key points
- *ensure records can be kept securely*
- *ensure all staff with access to such records are aware that information*

must not be given by them to unauthorized parties without the consent of the candidate, except as decreed by the awarding body
- *have a system in place that will guarantee the maintenance of secure and confidential storage.*

D343: Verify assessment practice

This involves the monitoring of assessment practice across a range of situations to national standards and the establishment of communications networks between assessors. If the process involved in D341 and D342 are being carried out effectively, this will ease the task of verifying assessments.

D343a) The eligibility of individuals to practise as assessors is checked against awarding body criteria

Explanation
Awarding bodies issue their own criteria for assessment practice which may detail additional or particular processes to be followed other than D32/33. Your external verifier will have details of how the awarding body's criteria will be monitored locally.

All assessors should either have a D32/33 unit award from TDLB or should be in the process of gaining one. This can be checked through registration and certification records, or by asking to see copies of certificates. Most awarding bodies also ask that the assessor is competent in the vocational area in which they will be assessing. Many awarding bodies hold their own training programmes for assessors on both the vocational skill and the training skill aspects of assessment. This can be a difficulty for some assessors, who are competent in a vocational area, have been used to assessing different types of programmes, and find it difficult to grasp the fact that the assessment process for NVQs/GNVQs has always to follow the processes for D32 and D33.

Key points
- *physically check assessor records and actions plans*
- *know the criteria required by the awarding body.*

D343b) Assessment practice and quality assurance arrangements are monitored in an appropriate proportion of instances to check that they meet awarding body requirements

Explanation
There will ideally be a rota or some other way of checking that the practice of all assessors is monitored regularly, and there will need to be a record of such monitoring. The primary purpose of monitoring is to ensure that systems are operating efficiently and effectively, not to question the professionalism and integrity of the staff involved. The practice of assessors will need

to be monitored through a combination of observation, questioning and examination of records, discussions, plans and spot checks. A lot of information will be able to be picked up in meetings, but this is obviously not the same as monitoring *practice.*

Guidance on assessment in general, and on units and elements in particular, will be given by the awarding bodies to which candidates and assessors are working. This guidance is often incorporated on to the pages on which the national standards are printed. Assessors will normally have two sets of guidance to work to: that provided by the awarding body giving the vocational qualification (e.g. CITB, Construction Industry Training Board), and that provided by the awarding bodies concerned with the vocational area of training and development, in relation to the relevant assessor and verifier awards.

Key points
- *ensure assessors are aware of the purpose of monitoring*
- *clarify with assessors how you will monitor practice*
- *agree with the external verifier what proportion of assessments should be monitored*
- *know where to find the awarding bodies' guidance on assessment*
- *understand that there may be two sets of guidance to follow.*

D343c) Assessors are given clear and constructive feedback

Explanation
Any monitoring assessments undertaken by internal verifiers with assessors should, of course, follow the procedures laid down in D32 and D33.

All assessors should receive feedback on their performance in the same way that this is given to any other candidate (see Chapter 3). The feedback will indicate areas of strength and areas for improvement. Areas for improvement (training needs) will no doubt be incorporated into training plans for individual assessors (see D341).

As long as you use the standards, procedures and documentation that you would expect your assessors to use, you shouldn't go wrong!

Key points
- *be positive with assessors*
- *ensure that assessors know how they are doing*
- *use the standards for assessment yourself!*

D343d) Judgements of evidence and assessment decisions are sampled regularly against the national standards to check their fairness and accuracy

Explanation
Whereas internal verification has sometimes been thought of as a straight

'systems check', this performance criteria emphasizes the 'moderation' aspect of the role. It is by the internal verifier looking carefully at the type of evidence being presented, and at the way in which assessors are judging that evidence, that consistency can be maintained across a centre, thus contributing to fair assessment. Sampling can be on a percentage basis or on some other basis agreed between the centre's staff. Meetings where assessors can all get together to make judgements on the same pieces of evidence are very helpful – eg, a videotape of a skills assessment, a GNVQ project, or a work placement report. Issues relating to subjectivity are bound to be raised, and such a session can focus the assessors (and the internal verifier) positively on the correct setting and interpretation of performance criteria.

Key points
- *give support and advice at the right time to minimize the risk of inconsistent judgements*
- *agree with the external verifier the degree of sampling that is needed*
- *compare evidence and assessment decisions to the relevant national standards.*

D343e) Documentation is complete, accurate and up-to-date

Explanation
It can be very easy to make a slip, eg, an incorrect spelling of a name or an incorrect birthdate and this will, in turn, cause unnecessary delays for candidates. Another more serious reason for checking for accuracy is to avoid the wrongful award of a certificate.

Candidates' log books and other work should be regularly seen, checked and completed by the assessors, which you need to check, and likewise, your *own* documentation needs to be regularly updated and checked for accuracy and completeness. See D342b and c.

Key points
- *check candidate's documentation*
- *check assessor's documentation*
- *check your documentation.*

D343f) Decision-makers are given clear explanations of the need for improvements in assessment practice

Explanation
As with any system, there will always, unfortunately, be those who try to circumvent it, and those who do not understand it and therefore act under misapprehensions. The NVQ assessment system has suffered from both problems. With the introduction of the revised standards, there is less scope for misinterpretation, but it remains of paramount importance that assessors and verifiers are rigorous in their practice. There must be good training for

assessors, a clear understanding by all concerned of the difference between delivery and assessment issues, adequate time provided for assessment, and realistic demands made of employers and candidates. The decision-makers involved need to understand the consequences of the actions or support that they give.

Key points
- *be able to state consequences clearly*
- *be aware of the need to maintain assessment standards to keep credibility for NVQs.*

D343g) Disputes and appeals are referred to the appropriate authority

Explanation
Disputes can be more common than you might think possible, particularly where interpretation of standards is concerned. There should be clear guidelines laid down in the submission made to the awarding body as to the normal procedure to be followed in such an event. All candidates and all assessors should be aware of the appeals procedure. The external verifier will be required to assist in matters relating to the interpretation of standards which cannot be resolved internally. Problems concerned with administration, eg, the delayed receipt of certificates, are likely to be the concern of the assessment centre or the awarding body, rather than the external verifier, whereas those relating to advice and training are likely to be the province of staff responsible for programme delivery. The internal verifier is likely to be the person involved in progressing any dispute or appeal.

Key points
- *have a clear, procedure for disputes and appeals*
- *ensure all involved are aware of the procedure*
- *ensure lines of responsibility are clear.*

D343h) Recommendations for awarding body action to maintain the quality of assessment are presented clearly and promptly to the external verifier

Explanation
The external verifier has a vital role to play in passing on information relating to the policies, interpretations and activities of the awarding body they represent. Likewise, the internal verifier needs to collate findings relating to assessment within the organization and pass these to the external verifier, whose job is then to pass on internal verifier's recommendations to the appropriate person, perhaps the regional verifier, for consideration. The sorts of evidence you will need are the minutes of team meetings held with assessors, notes of action points made and agreed with assessors as part of the monitoring process, and copies of requests for training or information to the

external verifier. You also need to keep records of any support that you have provided in the role of verifier, such as briefing, advising or coaching. Some regions have started assessor support networks which often discuss issues related to quality assurance; you should be aware of what is available for assessors and verifiers locally, regionally and nationally, and ensure that staff have access to as much information as possible.

Key points
- *keep notes of meeting and agreements with assessors to ensure accurate communication with the external verifier*
- *use the information given at local, regional and national level to inform assessors of required practice*
- *monitor assessor practice regularly across the range of assessment methods*
- *have clear guidelines to assist with disputes or appeals.*

	Original (Pre-Summer 1994)		Revised (Post-Summer 1994)
Unit D36	Identify previously acquired competence		Advise and support candidates to identify prior achievement
Element D361	*Help candidate to identify areas of current competence*		*Help the candidate to identify relevant achievements*
a	candidate is provided with clear and accurate information on the principles and implementation of accreditation of prior learning	a	the candidate is given clear and accurate information about the reasons for, and methods of, collecting and presenting evidence of prior achievement
b	support provided to candidate encourages a broad review of all pertinent experience	b	the candidate is encouraged to review all relevant experience
c	potential areas of current competence are accurately identified from a listing of experience	c	national standards which the candidate may potentially be able to achieve currently are accurately identified from the review of experience
d	style of support encourages self-confidence and self-esteem in candidate	d	support and the way it is given encourage self confidence and self-esteem in the candidate
e		e	options open to the candidate are explained clearly and constructively if the candidate expresses disagreement with the advice offered
	Range *Candidate:* young adult – mature adult; employed – unemployed; confident – non-confident; special needs *Sources of experience:* full-time employment; part-time employment; unpaid work; leisure activities; education and training		**Range** *1. Candidates:* young and mature adults; employed; unemployed; with special assessment requirements; with differing levels of confidence *2. Sources of experience:* paid work; unpaid work; leisure activities; education and training

	Original (Pre-Summer 1994)		Revised (Post-Summer 1994)
Element D362	*Agree an assessment plan with candidate*		*Agree and review an action plan for achieving qualifications*
a	realistic expectations and career aspirations are encouraged	a	candidates are given accurate advice and appropriate encouragement to enable them to form realistic expectations of the value and relevance of prior achievements
b	target vocational qualifications identified are appropriate to the candidate's current competence and future aspirations	b	target vocational qualifications identified are appropriate to candidate's prior achievements and future aspirations
c	advice to candidate accurately identifies units which might reasonably be claimed on the basis of existing competence	c	advice to the candidate accurately identifies unit(s) which might reasonably be claimed on the basis of prior achievement and evidence of continuing ability to achieve the element(s) within the unit(s)
d	opportunities to use evidence from prior achievements are accurately analysed	d	opportunities to use evidence from prior achievement are accurately analysed
c	assessment plans agreed with candidate provide an effective mix of evidence from prior achievements and current assessment	e	the plan agreed with the candidate identifies realistic actions to collect and present evidence of prior achievement efficiently
f	candidate motivation is encouraged throughout	f	the candidate's motivation and self-confidence is encouraged throughout
		g	if the candidate expresses disagreement with the advice offered, options open to the candidate are explained clearly and constructively
		h	the plan is reviewed appropriately with the candidate
	Range *Qualifications:* NVQ/SVQ levels 1–5; all occupational areas *Candidate:* young adult – mature adult; employed – unemployed; confident – non-confident; special needs		**Range** *1. Candidates:* young adults; mature adults; employed, unemployed; with special assessment requirements; confident; lacking in confidence

	Original (Pre-Summer 1994)		Revised (Post-Summer 1994)
Element D363	*Help candidate to prepare and present evidence for assessment*		*Help the candidate to prepare and present evidence for assessment*
a	candidate is provided with suitable support to prepare a portfolio of evidence	a	the candidate is provided with suitable support to prepare a portfolio of evidence
b	guidance provided to candidate during portfolio preparation encourages the development of clear, structured evidence relevant to the units being claimed	b	guidance provided to the candidate during portfolio preparation encourages the efficient development of clear, structured evidence relevant to the units being claimed
c	liaison with assessors establishes mutually convenient arrangements for review of portfolio and maintains the candidate's confidence	c	liaison with assessors establishes mutually convenient arrangements for review of portfolio and maintains the candidate's confidence
d	opportunities are identified for candidate to demonstrate competence where evidence from prior achievements is not available	d	opportunities are identified for the candidate to demonstrate achievement where evidence from prior experience is not available
e	awarding body documentation, recording and procedural requirements are met	e	awarding body documentation, recording and procedural requirements are met
		f	if there is disagreement with the advice given, options available to the candidate are explained clearly and constructively
	Range		**Range**
	Support: one-to-one; group; self study		*1. Support:* one-to-one; group; self study
	Portfolio content: direct evidence; indirect evidence; performance evidence; knowledge evidence		*2. Portfolio content:* evidence from naturally occurring opportunities; evidence from other opportunities; performance evidence; knowledge evidence
			3. Candidates: young and mature adults; employed, unemployed; with special assessment requirements; with differing levels of confidence

8 Guide to Unit D36: Advise and Support Candidates to Identify Prior Achievement

This unit covers the job role of the person who assists a candidate to identify prior achievements related to target vocational qualifications, and supports them in the compilation of portfolios of evidence, up to the point of assessment. Where possible, this role should be separate from that of the assessor, but in a very small organization the two roles may have to be undertaken by the same person. (Under no circumstances, however, can the assessor and the internal verifier be the same person.)

APL advisers need interpersonal skills to support candidates in the identification of needs, analysis and preparation phases of the process. They also need the ability to construct clear plans with candidates, not only for assessment paths and processes, but also for overall action. APL advisers should be familiar with the evidence requirements for the NVQs in which candidates are interested.

There are three elements to D36:

D361 – Help the candidate to identify relevant achievements
D362 – Agree and review an action plan for achieving qualifications
D363 – Help the candidate to collect and present evidence for assessment

D361: Help the candidate to identify relevant achievements

This element is concerned with helping candidates understand the APL process, and then to determine the areas in which they are currently competent. It is important that the adviser is able to present evidence which shows competence in dealing with a range of candidates, in particular young and mature adults, both in and out of paid work, who have differing levels of confidence.

D361a) The candidate is given clear and accurate information about the reasons for, and methods of, collecting and presenting evidence of prior achievement

Explanation
One of the big advantages of the NVQ system is that credit can be given for skills, knowledge and understanding previously acquired, provided that there is adequate evidence of achievement. This eliminates unnecessary training and instead, a candidate can concentrate specifically on areas of identified weakness. It is absolutely crucial that candidates are under no illusions about

APL, in terms of it being any easier than attending a traditionally taught and assessed programme. The onus is always on the *candidate* to present appropriate evidence, albeit with the adviser's support. They need to understand from the outset the system that the centre uses to support candidates, the differences between APL and traditional courses and assessment, and the costs that will be incurred, both in time and money. Some candidates may be suited to programmes other than APL because of their preferred learning styles, even though they may have considerable amounts of valid evidence. There is a range of printed and audio-visual material on the market that explains the APL process, which is useful when first meeting candidates, as well as books which deal comprehensively with the topic (see further reading).

Case study – a trainer in the prison service
Janice was a catering tutor in a young offender's institution. She had been working with candidates to NVQ level 2 in the large catering kitchen of the prison, and assessing against national standards was no problem. What was more of a problem was seeing a candidate through to the completion of a unit, as they tended to have erratic attendance or change institutions, and ensuring confidentiality regarding the candidates. Although Janice could have presented a lot of APL portfolio evidence, she decided to demonstrate her competence as an assessor through performance evidence observed in the workplace; she felt more confident there, preferred to be questioned orally and could refer to materials without removing them from the work environment.

Key points
■   *provide visual/written material about the APL process as a guide for candidates*
■   *ensure candidates are clear about what undertaking the process will mean for them.*

D361b) The candidate is encouraged to review all relevant experience

Explanation
Many candidates need help to review their work and non-work activities in order to build up a full picture of the skills, knowledge and experience they hold. A common misconception is that skills acquired through non-work or voluntary activities are 'not worth bothering about', particularly if they have no recognition in terms of certification. You may need to work hard with the client to develop an attitude of mind that looks positively at such experience. Support will undoubtedly be in the form of one-to-one guidance sessions, but you may also give help by providing diagnostic exercises on paper or through a computer program which take the candidate systematically through their relevant life experiences. A typical listing of a candidates experience gained through a review would include:

- planning and running a two-day public event
- budgeting for the same (no control of finance)
- control of household budget
- writing letters of complaint
- writing reports on community activities
- chairing meetings
- showing staff and visitors around the project
- using the computer for word-processing, including desk-top publishing
- telephone skills, including switchboard
- assisting with interviews for volunteers
- filing and devising filing systems
- organizing a baby-sitting circle.

Some candidates find it difficult to understand that for credit to be awarded they must be *currently* competent, eg although they may possess a typing qualification for example, they may no longer be able to type accurately at the required speed. A more difficult situation is where a candidate is convinced that they have enough evidence to gain an award, but has been working to very different standards from those required, or has lots of experience, but no evidence. It is therefore important that you and the candidate are aware that this part of the process is exploratory in nature and you, as adviser, will need to work sensitively with candidates.

Key points
- *check that the candidate is considering a full range of experience, including paid and unpaid work, leisure activities, education and training*
- *be able to offer a variety of support methods.*

D361c) National standards which the candidate may potentially be able to achieve currently are accurately identified from the review of experience

Explanation
The review you conduct with the candidate will give you a record of the candidate's experience to compare against national standards. From the information in the above example, a comparison of information could now be undertaken against national standards in the occupational area 'providing business services'. The identification of potential areas of competence must be accurate; in other words, taking account of the range of experience, you, as the adviser, should be able to make an initial assessment as to whether the candidates' experience can be matched against existing national qualifications. Sometimes a candidate may not have the eevidence for the award they are thinking of, but will satisfy the requirements of whole or part units of awards of which they were unaware. Adviser-candidates need to have knowledge of related NVQs and know who to contact if it appears that the candidate is more suited to a qualification with which they (the assessor-

candidate) are unfamiliar. The NVQ database provides information on all the qualifications.

Key points
- *be familiar with the evidence requirements of qualifications to ensure you give accurate advice.*

D361d) Support and the way it is given encourage self-confidence and self-esteem in the candidate

Explanation
The most important thing here is to make sure that the candidate has a positive goal at the end of this part of the process. The expectation may have initially been of a quick and simple certification route, or that there was maybe little point in considering APL. You will need to employ many of the skills used in counselling, which will allow the candidate to think through issues themselves, in an undisturbed atmosphere, with an empathetic adviser. If the candidate has low confidence (and this is often the case with, say, those returning to work after a career break, who may be doubting their ability to 'pick up where they left off', or to keep pace with younger employees), you will need to help the candidate to see the strengths they have built up through life experience and how these can be of help. It will also be important to work with the candidate to ensure that they will not feel let down if it transpires that APL will be able to play only a limited part in their progress towards accreditation. Likewise, candidates who have been made redundant may have feelings of low self-worth or esteem, and it can be helpful to concentrate on the transferability of skills in this context.

Key points
- *use appropriate interpersonal skills*
- *ensure facilities allow some degree of privacy*
- *work with the candidate to ensure that there will be some positive out-come, even if it is different from that initially anticipated.*

D361e) Options open to the candidate are explained clearly and constructively, if the candidate expresses disagreement with the advice offered

Explanation
Some candidates will want to go for APL regardless of the advice offered, or wish to pursue a particular NVQ when an alternative might be more suitable. It is important that you make them aware of possible consequences, such as only being able to achieve part of a qualification. The candidate and candidate-adviser should both be aware of the role of the centre's internal and external verifiers who may be able to give advice at this point. Chapters 3 and 5 give help in identifying and minimizing barriers to fair assessment.

Key points
- ensure the candidates' needs are taken into account
- use the centre appeals procedure when appropriate
- note down the candidates' options on their action plan.

D362: Agree and review an action plan for achieving qualifications

From the information gained in the first stage of the process, you now work with the candidate to devise an action plan for them to achieve a full qualification or unit(s), using evidence from prior achievements.

D362a) *Candidates are given accurate advice and appropriate encouragement to enable them to form realistic expectations of the value and relevance of prior achievements*

As mentioned already, candidates may have expectations relating to their prior experience which are either too high or too low. All achievements must be able to be corroborated in some way, perhaps through letters of validation (see fig 8.1) from previous employers, or through witness statements. Evidence relating to prior achievements, just like other forms of evidence, needs to fulfil the criteria of reliability, sufficiency, validity and authenticity, while contributing to the demonstration of the candidate's current competence. Candidates often overestimate the value of past qualifications and underestimate the value of life or work experience as a means of demonstrating competence.

Key points
- you need to demonstrate that you can work positively with the client, without raising false hopes
- you need to assess achievements accurately and realistically.

D362b) *Target vocational qualifications identified are appropriate to the candidate's prior achievements and future aspirations*

Explanation
It is at this stage that you need to discuss with the candidate their future plans, as it may be that *past* experiences will not help the candidate to progress along their desired path as much as their *current* competences. Sometimes candidates are better suited to gathering evidence at a quite different level or context from that which they first envisaged. Candidates who have had prior experiences in one area may well be able to provide relevant evidence, but want a change of direction. They will need advice on whether the unit(s) that they can claim through APL will be helpful to them in their future plans. They may also need help in determining which of several closely related unit qualifications best fits their evidence, eg, for a candidate who has done a lot

of work with cars, their evidence may be relevant to either electrical or vehicle body repair units.

Key points
- *you need to help the candidate to focus on future needs, as well as past experience*
- *you need to have an idea about the appropriateness of a candidate's past experience in relation to their aspirations.*

Dear Ms Tucker,

This is to confirm that Adrian Healey has worked for me for the past 4 years as my receptionist/assistant. During this time he:

> greeted all visitors, ensuring completion of the visitors' book and locating required staff;

> received and logged telephone calls;

> sorted and distributed incoming mail;

> sorted and franked outgoing mail;

> filed all documents;

> devised appropriate filing systems;

> maintained all office stock;

> ordered stock and dealt with suppliers;

> undertook all typing and preparation of graphical material as requested, using an IBM-compatible computer.

Adrian was also responsible for the supervision of occasional trainees in office skills work experience placements for reception, as well as organizing the two annual staff outings.

He has well-developed interpersonal skills, a comprehensive knowledge of the basics of office procedures and management and the ability to work on his own initiative.

All this work was performed to a competent, indeed, very satisfactory standard.

Yours sincerely

Susan Taylor

Figure 8.1 *Sample letter of validation*

D362c) Advice to the candidate accurately identifies unit(s) which might reasonably be claimed on the basis of prior achievement and evidence of continuing ability to achieve the element(s) within the unit(s)

Explanation

The important issue here is to focus on the claims that the candidate can make without any other training. The word 'reasonably' indicates that although there may be some small areas where the candidate might need to augment current competence to claim a complete unit (for example, they may need to collect more evidence to show consistency, or to provide full coverage of range statements) most of the evidence required can be provided through APL. This is where it will be necessary for the candidate to understand how to get valid evidence of past achievement and experience through the use of letters of validation from employers or colleagues.

You should be able to justify the advice you give to a candidate by using the standards to explain your assessment of their position.

Key points

- *a candidate may not be able to make use of all existing competence identified in making a claim*
- *letters of validation from employers must be comprehensive*
- *candidates need to be able to access additional evidence if needed.*

D362d) Opportunities to use evidence from prior achievement are accurately analysed

Explanation

It is important that achievements from APL identified by the two of you do fit the units identified as being able to be achieved. Sometimes a candidate will have identified a valid experience, for example, leading a group in an outdoor team-building activity, but the only way to get credit for the competence would be to repeat the exercise, at great expense. More often, candidates may possess evidence of achievements, but need help with understanding where this matches the standards. As the adviser, you will need to be able to assist the candidate to see the range of elements and criteria to which past achievements may relate. It is also very important to bear in mind when and how any achievement occurred. You will need to check that the methods learnt by the candidate are still in use, and that the skills or knowledge are not out of date. A common example is that of a trainer or teacher who possesses a valid Certificate of Education, taken perhaps seven years ago, who has been continuously employed on a part-time basis, and who wishes to gain an assessor's award. It is quite likely that they are very competent at assessing, and can produce evidence of marked work, but it is also likely that they have had no experience in assessing in a structured way against national standards, and may also know little or nothing about competence-based assessment. In this case you would have to help the candidate to see the limitations in their prior evidence, whilst looking for ways in which it might be used, such as in supplementary evidence, or to help cover the range of contexts required.

Key points
- *not all past experiences will be able to be used*
- *some past achievements will relate to several performance criteria or elements*
- *some past experiences may, while not being able to be used as the main body of evidence, be able to be used as supplementary or range evidence.*

D362e) The plan agreed with the candidate identifies realistic actions to collect and present evidence of prior achievement efficiently

Explanation
One of the biggest drawbacks to competence assessment through APL can be the amount of time it takes candidates to physically collect the evidence. The review you have undertaken together should have enabled you to analyse the sources of evidence needed to demonstrate prior achievement. The action plan needs clear time-scales and instructions.

Key points
- *plans need to guide candidates clearly, have realistic time-scales, and group similar actions together*
- *there needs to be a review mechanism built into the planning process.*

D362f) The candidate's motivation and self-confidence is encouraged throughout

For some candidates, a qualification may open the door to employment, whereas for others, the achievement may need to focus on self-satisfaction and the motivation to look more positively at voluntary or leisure opportunities. While both outcomes are equally valid, some candidates may find it helpful to read Charles Handy's *The Age of Unreason (1990)*, which examines the need to reassess our time as non-earners in a positive way, and helps the reader understand the need for diversification of skills in the workplace. It will be important to keep in regular contact with the candidate, in order to help them keep to schedule and to minimize demotivation. Get to know as much about the way your candidates work and study as possible; those with lower confidence will probably need more support (see also D361b and d).

Key points
- *keep in regular contact*

■   *be alert to signs of flagging enthusiasm or doubt.*

D362g) If the candidate expresses disagreement with the advice offered, options open to the candidate are explained clearly and constructively

Explanation
It is quite likely that the candidate will have their own ideas as to how to go about actioning the collection of evidence, and these ideas will probably be incorporated into the action plan (see also D362e). Options include contacting the internal verifier, abandoning APL, candidate progression but with the possibility of non-achievement, and a change of adviser. However, all these options should be suggested in a tactful way with the best interests of the candidate at heart. You need to be sure that the candidate's suggestions are considered carefully – they may be right!

Key point
■   *ensure the candidate understands the consequences of their actions.*

D362h) The plan is reviewed appropriately with the candidate

D363: Help the candidate to collect and present evidence for assessment

Whereas the two previous units have been concerned with identifying and analysing evidence, the focus of this unit is very much on the practicalities of assisting the candidate to prepare an evidence portfolio and on the arrangement of assessments.

D363a) The candidate is provided with suitable support to prepare a portfolio of evidence

Explanation
The candidate at this point will know what evidence, and in which forms, must be provided, because of the previous advice and analysis of evidence. It is likely that, having agreed an assessment plan, the candidate will now register with an appropriate awarding body and will therefore receive the documentation associated with the award. In most cases, this documentation will provide some guidance on how to proceed with the collection of evidence, but it is very likely that you, as the APL adviser, will need to help the candidate to interpret the standards and, in some cases, the guidance. The recent revision of the standards has hopefully reduced the amount of interpretation work for advisers, and there are a range of interactive and textual materials on the market (such as this book) aimed at giving additional sup-

port. Support will also mean access to materials, equipment, relevant people and sometimes study space, and you will no doubt wish to ensure that the candidate knows how to go about satisfying their needs in this respect. You will, by now, know enough about the candidate to know which is their preferred learning style. Ideally, there should be a range of means of support for the candidate to select from, ie, one-to-one, which will happen between yourself and the candidate; group sessions, where candidates can learn from and support each other; and materials for the candidate to work with alone in self-study. You will probably record these various choices and tasks on an action plan.

Key point
■   *check the range of the candidate's needs and that they know how to meet them.*

D363b) Guidance provided to the candidate during portfolio preparation encourages the efficient development of clear, structured evidence relevant to the units being claimed

Explanation
One of the most difficult tasks you have to do as an APL adviser is to guide candidates so that their evidence is in a form which both matches the standards required, and is presented in such a way that it is clear *why* it demonstrates competence. The portfolio should be immediately understandable to the assessor – indeed, one assessment centre tells its candidates that an assessor should be able to locate any piece of evidence within five seconds! Your portfolio, as adviser-candidate, needs to be accompanied by some evidence which explains *how* you guided the candidates to present acceptable evidence. Candidates have an uncanny knack of including evidence which is irrelevant to the unit they are wishing to claim. You will need to develop the ability to detect irrelevancies and persuade candidates to remove them! Again, *how* you do this will need to be explained in your portfolio. Clear, structured, evidence is likely to be well referenced, simply arranged and the candidate will have collected items of evidence which each cover a range of elements and performance criteria. The candidate will need to understand the performance criteria, range statements and knowledge and understanding specifications *well* before they can do this without a lot of guidance.

Key points
■   *you need to demonstrate that you can give all three types of support, ie, one-to-one, group and self-study*
■   *there needs to be evidence of how you deal with the varying needs of candidates*
■   *you need to present records of assisting and advising one candidate (plus two portfolios – original standards).*

D363c) Liaison with assessors establishes mutually convenient arrangements for review of portfolio and maintains the candidate's confidence

Explanation
The candidate needs to feel that the assessment process to come will be a rewarding, if challenging, experience, and as the candidate's adviser you will endeavour to maintain constructive and friendly links with assessors, which will help to create a positive assessment climate for the candidate. Often, the adviser will introduce candidate and assessor before the portfolio review, so that the assessor can add to or agree the assessment plan for the actual portfolio review. If you have supported the candidate in an appropriate manner so far, they are likely to have a good level of confidence about the acceptability of their evidence, and it is important that they maintain a positive approach at this stage.

Key points
- *show how you liaise with assessors to their and the candidate's mutual satisfaction*
- *demonstrate that you use interpersonal skills which maintain the candidate's confidence.*

D363d) Opportunities are identified for the candidate to demonstrate achievement where evidence from prior experience is not available

Explanation
During the process of devising the action plan (D362), you will have identified the areas where, although competent, the candidate has inadequate evidence to present from past experience. You now need to work with assessors to arrange opportunities for the candidate to demonstrate competence in either a real work or simulated environment. There will no doubt be documentation to complete which explains the actions you take to do this. Large centres are likely to have well-equipped training workshops where time, resources and facilities for feedback after the assessment are available. Assessment of competence in this way can be costly if not carefully thought out so that an assessment opportunity covers a maximum number of competences in as short a time as possible.

Key points
- *discuss how candidates can demonstrate previously-acquired competence in a practical way*
- *be aware of the real and simulated environments where competence can be assessed.*

D363e) Awarding body documentation, recording and procedural requirements are met

Explanation
This is straightforward enough. Throughout the whole time of supporting a candidate, the adviser must make sure that not only are careful records kept which identify the decisions made, and feedback undertaken with candidates, but also that any particular requirements of awarding bodies are followed. These may range from the completion of personal learning journals to the adherence to equal opportunities policies.

Key points
- *ensure that you are completing the required documentation satisfactorily*
- *ensure that you understand the processes relating to particular awarding bodies.*

D363f) If there is disagreement with the advice given, options available to the candidate are explained clearly and constructively

See D361e) and 362g).

Section 3

9 Evidence and Action Planning

Types of evidence

Some key ideas on evidence have already been covered in Chapter 1, and the step-by-step guide for your particular award should have provided you with sufficient knowledge of the performance criteria. Help and advice on appropriate evidence and any extra training needed should be available to you. However, it should be you, the candidate, who decides what evidence to use, how you are going to collect it and the time-scale involved. This chapter is intended to help *you* – the candidate for an assessor, verifier or APL adviser award – by giving information about different types of evidence, clarifying the evidence you might wish to use and providing you with examples of how you can plan for this evidence collection.

Direct and indirect evidence

Broadly speaking, evidence can be divided into two types: direct and indirect evidence. *Direct* evidence is evidence which can be directly observed by the person assessing or which has been directly produced by the candidate. This could mean watching a candidate groom a horse, plaster a wall, install part of a heating system, handle a difficult employee – in fact any situation where an activity, process or procedure is being performed. For a candidate wishing to provide evidence for the assessor's award, direct evidence could be provided by being observed performing an assessment. Another possible form of direct evidence is the product that has actually been produced by the candidate – a shoe that has been manufactured, an assignment that has been written, the completed hair style of a client. In the assessor's award, this product could take on a number of different characteristics; for example, a written feedback sheet, a completed candidate record or a memo sent to the internal verifier could all be 'products'.

Indirect evidence involves a third party of some kind, ie, other than the official assessor and the candidate. The evidence of a candidate's employer confirming that they have seen the candidate perform a certain activity or procedure would involve the employer as the third party. In the assessor's award, a line manager who had worked alongside the candidate and observed them assessing might be prepared to give a written witness statement to confirm that the candidate never used leading questions and passed on the results of the assessment promptly to the appropriate person. In this case the line manager would be the third party. Another type of third party might not be a person at all, but a certificate or qualification obtained by the candidate which confirmed that they were competent in a particular area. In the assessor's awards, for example, some City and Guilds trainers awards provide third party evidence that the candidate is likely to be competent in most of the elements in D32.

Three methods of producing evidence

1. Performance evidence

This type provides evidence that you are currently able to perform particular aspects of a role within an occupational area, by an accredited assessor observing you actually carrying it out. Performance evidence can also be the result of the 'performance', ie, the product or products you have produced as a result of performing the particular task or skill. These 'products' could be a manufactured article or a successfully completed installation or repair. Although 'product' is an impersonal term, an assessment for a candidate in an NVQ in child care and education working with a group of obviously happy and well cared-for children would take into account the successful 'products' of the work he or she is performing. The products you might produce could be documents you use for recording interviews or tutorials, assignments you have written towards a qualification, etc.

The best kind of performance evidence is that which arises naturally from your work situation, but there may be occasions where simulation in the form of specially designed tasks or role plays is necessary, eg, in a situation where a candidate might have to demonstrate competence in emergency procedures. For those working towards the assessor/verifier/APL adviser awards, simulation will probably be used very little, as all candidates for these awards should be covering most competences as part of their normal work and where they are not, questioning would probably be the most likely way of ensuring that the range is covered.

In the assessor/verifier/APL adviser awards, as in other awards, as much evidence as possible should be generated through being directly observed, eg, an APL adviser-candidate being observed conducting several advice sessions by their official assessor will probably have produced much of the evidence needed for the award. An assessor-candidate being observed planning assessments with a number of different candidates and being observed giving feedback would also produce a substantial amount of evidence.

2. Supplementary evidence

As it suggests, this is evidence to supplement any gaps in the evidence that has been generated through direct observation. Most importantly, this is the evidence that you will provide to show that you have the required knowledge and understanding. This can be provided through your assessor asking you a series of questions, by having to sit a written test or by writing an explanation of your understanding of a particular process or area of knowledge. For example, someone working towards the internal verifier's award (D34) may

Source of evidence	Assessed by	Advantages	Disadvantages
Natural performance	Direct observation of you at work Examining end product	Current Can cover large number of elements and performance criteria if planned well Convenient (if part of your normal work) No problem with authenticity if you are actually seen performing	Can be costly in assessor time if assessor and candidate work in different places You may have to arrange to do something specially to fit in with your assessor's availability You may perform less well due to 'nerves' Possibly disruptive to colleagues
Performance in specially set tasks or situations	Simulations: • role plays • assignments • projects, etc	Current Enables you to demonstrate competence in performance criteria or range you may not be able to cover in the workplace Controlled situation or task	Can be difficult to construct a realistic simulation You may underperform because the situation is 'artificial' If tasks, projects, etc. are not carefully designed, you may not meet all the required performance criteria Projects and assignments may only provide evidence of written skills at the expense of performance
Questioning	Oral tests Written tests Essay questions Full assignments or projects	Can be a quick way to provide evidence Can support other evidence by providing context and depth Oral questioning can be done as part of the observation Written tests can ensure coverage of range, knowledge and understanding	You may be nervous at being 'tested' You may misunderstand the questions You may have to use written skills that are not necessarily appropriate to your competence at work
Historical	Evidence from prior experience, achievement or learning	Can save time, if you have wide variety of relevant experiences and have them well-documented and organized Can provide evidence of knowledge and understanding Can provide evidence of range not covered by current situation	The evidence may not be current for today's working standards Matching it against the standards could be more time-consuming than actually demonstrating competence in other ways It may be difficult to prove that it is authentic It may take time chasing up evidence. eg, letters from previous employers

Figure 9.1 *Advantages and disadvantages of different types of evidence*

write an account of what they understand by verification and how verification works within their own organization. Someone working towards their assessors' awards may wish to convince their official assessor that they have a good background knowledge of assessment, so they may include a description of different types of assessment they have used in the past together with some evaluation of their strengths and weaknesses.

3. Evidence from prior achievements or prior experience

This can be provided from a number of different sources. For example, letters of validation from credible witnesses to your competence such as previous employers and clients, or reports from third parties on work in which you have had direct involvement. One candidate that we assessed had been working in a glass-making factory and had been involved in producing a large report involving assessment of health and safety procedures within his workplace. Another candidate was working in a college of further education and was able to produce a report from the Further Education Funding Council which had monitored her department and which specifically praised the GNVQ pilot programme she had run. An assessor-candidate could produce third party evidence from an external verifier's report which praised the quality of assessment practice in their section or from a line manager, witnessing that they had been assessing effectively for a number of years. Evidence can also be provided from certificates and qualifications gained in the past proving that you have the relevant experience and competence. However, in all of these cases, the *currency* of competence is an important factor and if there is any doubt of your ability to perform to current national standards then your assessor will probably want to observe you directly to confirm that you really are competent.

Prior achievements, particularly where you have done written work such as essays or assignments or produced training materials, are often useful for providing evidence of the knowledge and understanding required. A candidate for the assessor's awards who had completed an initial teacher or trainer training qualification such as the Certificate in Education for the post-16 sector would certainly have covered assessment during those programmes and may have kept written evidence of that fact.

Looking at your own work context

Each of these types of evidence has its own advantages and disadvantages and you may need to ask for help and advice over which evidence you will use. However, a useful starting point in the planning process to determine the strongest, easiest-to-produce and most cost-effective evidence is to begin with your current place of work and job role. Consider whether assessment, verification and APL advice normally take place within your own organization and, if so, how they occur. This is extremely important, because it will enable you to build on what arises naturally from your own work instead of manufacturing an alien system of processes and procedures purely for the sake of achieving the award. In our experience, candidates who have tried to do this have felt the assessment process is mechanical paper-gathering and have not understood or felt any ownership of the procedures involved. Unfortunately, the potential knock-on effect is that assessors who have no belief in the quality of the assessment process, and who have not found this experience useful and meaningful themselves, are unlikely to pass on much motivation or enthusiasm to their own candidates. Some useful questions to ask at this point are:

- How does assessment take place within my own work situation?
- What procedures, if any, are already in place for monitoring and recording assessment?
- What procedures do we have, if any, for verifying the assessment?
- How do we usually test what someone knows and understands in my area of work?
- What different situations and contexts described in the range for the award are normally covered?
- Are there any APEL procedures already in place?

In order to individualize the process and enable it to genuinely reflect the assessment practice that arises from your own work situation, let us consider the different work contexts where assessment might take place.

How does assessment take place in my own work situation?

Different work situations will sit more comfortably with different types of assessment. Although there will obviously be exceptions, it is likely that the following are fairly representative.

Schools
These will have well-established assessment and verification systems. Assessment will traditionally be based on written evidence from essays, tests or assignments. Assessments should be documented and eventually lead towards formal qualifications. In the past, assessments will have been biased towards academic rather than vocational ability.

Colleges
These will also have well-established assessment and verification systems, again biased towards written evidence but with more opportunities for performance evidence to be used. Assessments should be documented and generally lead towards formal qualifications. Assessments will be academically or vocationally oriented.

Large organizations
In most large organizations there will be well-established employee

assessment systems usually linked to a staff appraisal system. These systems will be based on performance evidence, assessing how effectively individuals are carrying out their work roles and what the resultant training and development needs might be. Formal appraisal systems will be documented and there may be progress reports on individual employees, particularly those undergoing specific training. Informal assessments may be taking place on a continuous basis, particularly with trainees, and will probably take the form of a line manager or supervisor 'keeping an eye' on a trainee to see if they can do the job. In-house training will probably not be formally assessed, although employees may have been supported to obtain formal qualifications elsewhere.

Small organizations
These will probably have continuous informal assessment of employees based on performance evidence, ie, how someone is actually doing their job. For example, the owner of a small garage with a new trainee mechanic will probably be working in the same work area and making regular mental notes of what the trainee can or cannot do (ie, the areas where they are competent or not competent), where he or she needs to be shown how to do something properly and where they can be trusted to do something completely on their own. However, it is unlikely that these assessments will be documented and there is unlikely to be any formal assessment of their performance. Obviously, an exception to this would be if the trainee had come to the garage as part of a Youth Training programme and the employer would be giving formal feedback to an outside work placement visitor from this programme. In small organizations, employees may have been supported to obtain a formal qualification elsewhere, perhaps on a day-release basis.

From these descriptions you will probably be able to identify the situation nearest to your own. You can then ask yourself the next question.

What procedures are already in place for monitoring and recording assessment?

Once you have identified what type of assessment normally takes place within your own organization, you will then be able to decide on the next step. You need to identify whether your part in these assessment activities is likely to fulfil the evidence requirements for all the relevant elements, performance criteria, range, knowledge and understanding without calling on any other sources of evidence. Whether you think there are a number of existing procedures or you think you are starting without a formal assessment structure, it might be useful to recall the stages of the assessment process given in Chapter 1 and identify what documents might be needed to record these stages. More details on some of these documents will be given later in this chapter.

Stages of the assessment process – possible types of documentation

- Planning: awarding body guidelines, details of units and elements being covered, action plans, assessment plans, assignment briefing sheets
- Collecting evidence: action plans, assessment plans, interview or tutorial records, records of action planning interviews, handouts giving guidelines on evidence
- Making judgements: awarding body guidelines, assessment plans, observation checklists, bank of questions, written tests, minutes of meetings with other assessors ensuring consistency in judgements
- Giving feedback: feedback sheets – formative and summative, interview/tutorial records
- Recording decisions: summative assessment sheets, candidates' log books, overall summary sheet of units achieved, official awarding body documentation recording candidates' achievements.

At this stage, you may find you have all or a substantial amount of the necessary documentation, in which case completed examples of the relevant forms will provide you with much of the necessary product evidence. If your organization does not have this documentation, then you may find that the awarding body you are using will already have devised some which you can use or adapt if required. Alternatively, you may decide to design some that are specific and appropriate to your own work context. It is important to emphasize that in a situation like this, relevant documentation will be necessary if you are to set up a workable system to assess NVQs or GNVQs, but it should be documentation that you feel 'fits' the way your organization works.

What procedures do we already have in place for recording the verification process?

Organizations which already have verification systems will probably administer and record them in different ways. For NVQs and GNVQs, it will be essential for internal verifiers to have access to a copy of the awarding body's guidelines and also a copy of all the units and elements being assessed. Also documentation is needed to record:

- observation of assessors
- portfolios that have been internally verified (with comments)
- visits from and discussions with external verifiers
- dates, times and subjects of meetings with named assessors.

For organizations which do not have formal verification systems, the step-by-step guide to D34 will give some indication of what is required.

What are the most natural ways of testing knowledge and understanding within this work context?

Although there may be occasions, for example, when an individual in a position of responsibility in a commercial or industrial organization is required to write a report where their knowledge and understanding of a particular aspect of work will be demonstrated, it is unlikely that actual written testing would normally be used in this work context. The most natural method of testing knowledge or understanding would be to question employees while they are actually performing the work. This would check that they are clear what they are doing and that they have a proper understanding of what is involved. If the questioning needed to probe any deeper, a separate discussion might take place where the employee was questioned further, perhaps to elicit ideas on what they would do if a particular situation occurred or if they had to perform the work in a different context – in other words, questioning across the range, and covering a variety of contingencies.

There is a contrast between this work context and one such as a school or a college where some form of written testing would be part of the normal expectations of being in such an environment. Although oral testing on an ongoing basis would be part of the process of formative assessment, most students would expect to have to prove knowledge and understanding through written means at various points in the programme. When deciding the most appropriate ways of testing, it is therefore important to consider what is least disruptive to your own candidates, and formulate ways of testing that are most likely to elicit answers which provide a genuine reflection of what they know and understand.

Certain awarding bodies for NVQs do specify at least one written test, and GNVQs have a written end test as well as written evidence produced on an ongoing basis throughout the programme. The evidence on testing knowledge and understanding that you produce for your assessors awards might include one or more of the following:

- a bank of questions that you use for oral testing
- examples of written tests that you use
- examples of assignments or projects identifying the elements and performance criteria being assessed.

Is all the range covered?

Candidates for the assessors' awards are often covering all the range, without realizing it, perhaps because they are not doing it consistently or systematically. For example, one assessor-candidate working in the vehicle body area did not think he was covering the range *candidate and peer assessment* because he was not doing this on a formal basis. However, he was asking his vehicle body candidates what they thought of their own work and he was getting other vehicle body candidates to comment on each other's work.

Once this was pointed out to him, he began to do this in a more systematic fashion and to record the comments as they were made. The evidence was already there; he just needed to realize this and structure it more consistently. This also had the effect of improving his own assessment practice, as he made sure that everyone had the opportunity to give and receive feedback and ideas for improvements. Where all the range is not covered, you need to work out whether you would be able to cover the range by reorganizing your work, for example by 'swapping' candidates with a colleague. If not, then you should discuss with your adviser or assessor the most appropriate way you could demonstrate specific aspects of the range, possibly by answering a number of pre-set questions, e.g. What if ... ? questions.

Sources of evidence and specifications for evidence

A number of different sources of evidence have already been mentioned. The list below, although by no means comprehensive, may provide some ideas on the variety of evidence that is possible, both from your present work role and from previous experience or achievements. The evidence might be used to demonstrate competence against the performance criteria in the assessor awards. Some evidence may be used to demonstrate knowledge and under-standing and to cover the range. The list also includes suggestions on ways of demonstrating that the evidence meets the requirements of authenticity, validity and currency. Remember, you do not need a vast amount of evidence, just evidence of the right kind.

Evidence	Specification
action plans	completed and signed
agendas of meetings	your name highlighted, put in context
APL documents	completed and signed
appraisal records	your name highlighted, key points highlighted
assessment plans	completed and signed
assignments	clear indication of elements and performance criteria covered
audio tapes of briefings	labelled, indication of elements and performance criteria covered
awarding body guidelines	areas highlighted if appropriate
briefing notes	witnessed, put in context
checklists	completed and signed
candidate record cards	official heading, dated
certificates	originals
charts	clear indication of where they can be seen, eg, wall of my office
core skills logs	completed, signed

costings	official paper or witnessed
diaries	put in context, key points highlighted if appropriate
direct observation	time, date, place, purpose, elements and performance criteria identified, signed by observer, official position of observer stated
equal opportunities policy	areas highlighted where appropriate
feedback sheets	completed, signed, official heading if appropriate
flow charts	purpose identified
forms	completed
graphs	put in context, explained
induction documents	key areas highlighted
job specifications	key points highlighted
lesson plans	relevant areas highlighted
letters of validation	covering specific elements/performance criteria,signed, official position of validator stated, official paper, date they knew you stated
log books	completed, signed
memos	your name highlighted
minutes of meetings	your name highlighted or attendance witnessed
photographs	officially captioned or witnessed, put in context
projects	clear identification of elements and performance criteria covered
publicity material	key areas highlighted, explained
qualifications	original certificates, explanation of their relevance
questions to test knowledge and understanding	clear indication of what elements they cover, indication of whether they require oral or written answers
questionnaires	completed, put in context
record sheets	completed, signed if appropriate
references	your name highlighted, explanation of relevance
reports	your name highlighted, relevance explained
rotas	your name highlighted, key areas highlighted
schemes of work	key points highlighted
software	type of machine it runs on, sample print-out

testimonials	covering specific elements/performance criteria, signed, official position of person stated
timesheets/tables	your name/key areas highlighted
tutorial sheets	completed, signed if appropriate
verifiers' reports	signed
videos	clearly labelled, clear identification of elements and performance criteria covered.

Devising an action plan

In planning the evidence needed, it is advisable to produce some form of action plan, which is a means of planning what evidence is going to be presented for assessment and is usually produced as a result of the candidate having a meeting with the person acting as their adviser. This adviser can be an APL adviser, who is there specifically to help the candidate prepare evidence from prior experience or the adviser can be the person who will later carry out the formal assessment, but at present is acting in the advisory role. Action planning could take place on a long-term basis, ie, 'What do you need to do to obtain the whole qualification?' or it may take place in separate stages, eg, unit by unit.

There are no right or wrong formats for an action plan, although they all probably share some common characteristics – they identify appropriate evidence, they describe how that evidence will be presented, they indicate what the candidate needs to collect or arrange and they set some kind of targets for completion, including an indication of the time-scale involved. These targets are agreed between the candidate and adviser and can form the basis of a review at the next meeting. Action planning can be a purely informal process whereby the candidate merely makes a mental note of what they need to do after discussing it with their adviser. However, because of the need to ensure that the candidate is really clear about what evidence is appropriate and what they need to do to provide it, action plans are often formally agreed and documented.

NB. Action plans are sometimes combined with assessment plans. For more details on these, see the section later in this chapter.

Strategies for the collection of evidence

Through your action plan, you will have identified the evidence that needs to be collected together. This is the point where candidates for the awards often feel rather overwhelmed because this stage involves gathering together documents, getting people to write letters of validation, getting people to witness that you have performed certain tasks and organizing to be observed, where appropriate to the award. The following points might help.

ACTION PLANNING FLOWCHART

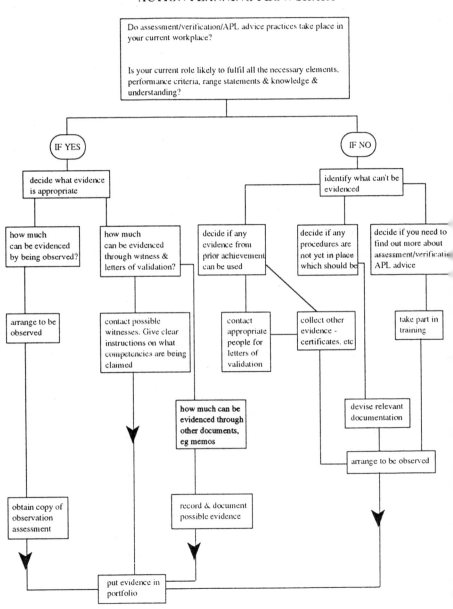

Figure 9.2 *Action planning flow chart*

Familiarize yourself with the units you are trying to achieve

In this way, you have an overview of what evidence is needed and can be alert to opportunities to provide that evidence. You will also be able to see if that evidence can be cross-referenced to cover other elements.

Make the most of performance evidence

It is possible to demonstrate a large number of competences at one time if organized correctly. Work out beforehand what you could evidence through being observed and plan your assessor's visit accordingly.

Organize your documents

Individuals have their own systems for organizing themselves and we would not want to be prescriptive as there is no single 'correct' way to organize a portfolio. However, if you have no idea where to start, this is a system which some people have used successfully. Get an A4 ring binder and cardboard sections and number these according to the separate elements. As you gather together each piece of evidence, put it straight into the binder. In this way, you can keep a check on what you still need to collect. Make an index system at the front for ongoing reference and make notes to indicate which performance criteria are covered by each piece of evidence (see Chapter 10).

Obtain letters of validation or witness statements where necessary

Letters of validation are written documents which confirm (validate) the candidate's claim to competence in particular areas. The main problem that arises when these are produced as evidence is that they are too general. You should prepare the person writing the letter as to exactly what is required, ie, exactly which elements or performance criteria you are hoping that they will validate. A slightly less formal way of validating someone's competence is a witness or testimonial statement, again related to specific competences, which usually takes the form or a written or typed statement signed by an appropriate person. Make sure that, in all these cases, the official position of the person confirming your competence is identified, eg, R Jones, Personnel Manager, Crace Engineering Ltd (see specimen letter in Chapter 8).

Maximize evidence

Make sure you are making the most out of every piece of evidence you use. When getting a line manager to write a witness statement, think if they can witness anything else at the same time. When being observed make sure you evidence as much as possible. When considering any piece of evidence, think whether it could also evidence any other competences.

Agreeing an assessment plan

Through discussions with your adviser, you should have identified which

Assessment Activity Action Plan		For: Prepared with:	Name (Learner) J.Stone		
			Name (Tutor) P.Wells		
			Centre Cawville College		

What do I need to find out?	What do I need to do?	In which order?	By when?	Have I achieved it?
How day centre for elderly funded	Arrange interview with community worker with the elderly	4	27/1/94	No
Laws about provision for elderly	Arrange interview with Mrs Marriott who runs the day centre	3	27/1/94	Yes
How funding has changed in last ten years	Read section in textbook on legal provision for elderly	1	20/1/94	Yes
How facilities have changed	Research back copies of relevant magazines	2	20/1/94	Yes
Attitudes of staff and users to standard of facilities at present	Compose set of questions for 1) Mrs Marriott 2) staff 3) users 4) community worker	5	3/2/94	1) yes 2) yes 3) yes 4) no

Tutor comment	Review Dates
You are working well and have organized your time efficiently. Perhaps it would have been a good idea to have asked for an alternative name to contact when you knew the community worker was away	4/2/94

Figure 9.3 *Detail from a BTEC GNVQ assessment activity sheet*

units you are working towards and what evidence is required. The assessment plan takes this a stage further and actually identifies a time and a place when you will be assessed on specific elements and performance criteria. NB. Sometimes the action plan and assessment plan are included in the same document; see the samples of different assessment plans in Figures 9.3 and 9.4.

Arranging a workplace assessment

Chapter 3 gives some detail about observation in the workplace from the observer's point of view. From a candidate's point of view, you need to make sure that you make the most of this to demonstrate competences across the range. For example, a candidate for the APL adviser's award could arrange to be observed conducting a series of APL interviews on the same afternoon including ones with a mature unemployed adult and a young employed adult, one confident, one unconfident, one on an initial interview and one at an interview where the portfolio was almost complete. Other points you need to consider carefully include how you will introduce the assessor to anyone else who might be present, where the assessor should sit or stand and whether you need to brief them on anything before you begin.

ASSESSMENT PLAN McLasky Training

Name: *Gordon Roberts*

Programme: *NVQ in Retailing*

Units and elements for assessment:

Unit 201 Providing a service to the customer

Element 201.1 Establish contact with customer
p.c. 1-4

Element 201.2 Respond to customer requests
p.c. 1-7

Topic:

Evidence for presentation:

1. *Observation at work placement serving customers. 21st March. 2-4 pm*
2. *Report from supervisor at work placement on how effectively customers are dealt with covering all p.c. and aspects of range not covered through observation*
3. *Answers to questions on company policies and Trades Descriptions Act after observation*

Action plan:

Gordon - make sure Mr Armitage, the owner of the shop knows about the assessment on Thursday 21st March
Find out about Trades Descriptions Act

J Ellis - will make sure Mr Armitage knows what should be covered - the report

Time, date and place of assessment: *Thursday 21st March. 2-4 pm*

Time, date and place of feedback: *Thursday 21st March. 4-5 pm*

Joint signatures of agreement: *Gordon Roberts* | *J Ellis (Assessor)*

Figure 9.4 *Assessment plan and action plan combined*

Make sure you have agreed on what is to be assessed and that both you and the assessor have a copy of any notes taken during the observation. You can use these as evidence in your portfolio.

Summary

After reading this chapter you should be aware of:

- types of evidence related to assessor/verifier/adviser awards
- assessment practice in your own place of work
- advantages and disadvantages of different types of evidence
- different sources of evidence for the assessor/verifier/adviser awards
- action plans and assessment plans.

10 Presentation of your Portfolio of Evidence

Organization; formats for presentation; organizing your evidence; checking evidence against the standards; indexing and cross-referencing; linking evidence to performance criteria; putting the evidence in context; a final word.

Organization

There are no requirements laid down in the standards on how you should present evidence, although there may be some guidance in the materials produced by the awarding body with whom you are registering.

The portfolio

Candidates will eventually submit performance evidence, ie, evidence drawn from current practice, including observations of assessment, evidence from prior experience, including letters of validation and witness statements, and supplementary evidence, eg, to support knowledge and understanding, or to support areas where performance evidence cannot be provided. This collection of materials will normally be presented for assessment in a file or folder, suitably referenced, which is then commonly known as 'the portfolio'. A familiar example of a portfolio of evidence is the portfolio produced by an art student, which consists of samples of their work, usually in a variety of media; some evidence may consist of written descriptions or photographs if the work is, for example, performance art or a large sculpture. Other examples are an actor's portfolio, representing the range of roles played, and the portfolios held by cabinet ministers, which are the range of activities and responsibilities expected of them. The point is that your portfolio is likely to be a collection of mixed evidence, some of which may not be easily or sensibly translated into written form; the 'portfolio' presented for assessment will, however, indicate where such evidence can be found or corroborated.

Presentation

The major considerations influencing presentation are as follows:

- the specific requirements of the awarding body with which you register
- the time (and therefore cost) at your disposal for assessment. The more things you explain clearly in writing, the fewer verbal checks your assessor will need to make, thus saving time. Only you can assess the relative costs to yourself of having a lot of practical workplace

assessment rather than providing supplementary evidence of prior achievement

- the clarity with which your evidence is displayed and explained, especially concerning indexing and linking of your evidence to the performance criteria
- the inclusion of relevant evidence only. Bulk, in evidence, as with candidates or assessors, is no indicator of quality or competence!

It is helpful if the material is presented in a way that is physically easy to handle – ring binders are generally easier than box or wallet files in this respect. Until recently, one awarding body used to supply a ring binder and plastic wallets as part of the standards pack. An assessor's nightmare is the evidence for a couple of units which takes up two lever arch files and a document wallet, and showers bits of referencing papers onto the floor as it is wrestled from triple wrapping liberally covered with sellotape!

Accessibility and legibility

Since there are no standard rules for organizing the portfolio, a good rule of thumb is that your portfolio will probably be acceptable if someone unfamiliar with your work can understand the layout and the way that evidence relates to the standards. Ask a colleague or friend to look through it, and see whether they can find specific pieces of evidence within, say, five seconds. Devising a simple referencing system is *really important*, as is completing accurately any evidence summary lists, or other documentation required by the awarding bodies. Most candidates opt for a ring binder containing plastic wallets into which can be slipped different types of evidence, from papers to videotapes. The advantage of this system is that you can, without damaging

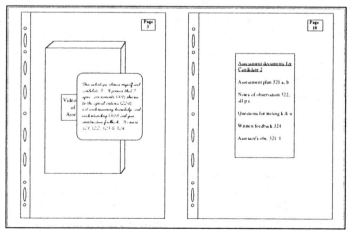

Figure 10.1 *Two examples of labelled evidence wallets*

the evidence itself, easily reference it and write explanations on it by putting sticky labels on the wallets, or by slipping more substantial written explanations inside the wallets.

There is no necessity to have everything typed. Much of your evidence is likely to be in the form of proformas completed by hand while observing or interviewing candidates, or other types of working documents such as memoranda, and it would be inappropriate to alter these. However, all handwritten evidence must be legible, particularly if it is to be read by candidates or staff involved with the assessment process, but unless your handwriting is appalling, or you are able to type your own material, the costs involved in asking others to process your original text will probably outweigh the benefits. If you have video or audiotape material, the sound quality should be reasonable, and there should also be some way for the assessor to easily and quickly find specific items on the tape. Similarly, photographs need to be clearly labelled. The way that you prepare your own portfolio and the documentation you devise will probably be useful in helping you to develop a method and standard of portfolio presentation which can be a model for your trainee candidates.

Formats for presentation

The standards will have been given to you along with various items of supporting material from the awarding bodies and possibly some centre-devised documentation. Wherever possible, it is a good idea to utilize these materials to form a framework for the presentation of your own evidence – after all, you or your organization will have paid for them! It will normally be necessary to separate out the copies of the standards themselves, all documentation requiring completion by the assessor and the candidate, and any useful dividers supplied with the standards pack. A format that has been found helpful is as follows:

General points
- label the portfolio clearly, on both the front and the spine, with your name, the units you are claiming and your organization (if relevant). This seems obvious but is omitted by a surprising number of candidates
- ensure that everything is secure, and that nothing is likely to fall out or drop off.

Introduction
- a contents page, and a clear explanation of how to access the evidence, right at the front
- all awarding body documents requiring the signatures of yourself or your assessor. These will include records of achievement and composite or summary evidence sheets
- a brief description of your role (a targeted CV) relating to advising

candidates on APL, assessment, or verification, depending on the awards you are claiming
■ statements relating to your competence in your vocational area, eg, construction, computing.

Process
■ action plans showing the tasks undertaken during the collection of evidence
■ learning journals, or learning statements, if required by the awarding body.

Evidence
■ performance, supplementary and APL, all indexed and referenced.

Organizing the evidence

You will have to make some decisions about how to arrange your evidence. There are several ways of doing this; here are some examples:

Example A
■ gathering together the evidence relating to separate elements and arranging it in sequence, eg, all the evidence for D321, then D322, etc.

Example B
■ presenting discrete items of evidence which may refer to several units and elements, eg, a set of materials which relate to a complete assessment process with a particular candidate.

Example C
■ sorting evidence according to origin, eg, evidence from prior achieve-

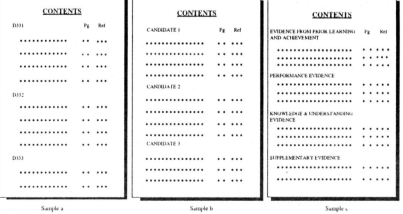

Figure 10.2 *Examples showing three ways of presenting evidence*

ments, performance evidence, evidence of knowledge or understanding, supplementary evidence.

Cross-referencing and indexing against the standards

Your action plan or assessment plan should have enabled you to collect appropriate evidence cross-referenced and indexed against specific performance criteria. You may have inadvertently collected some evidence which does not directly relate to the units in question, but of which you are proud and consequently want to present, or because you had an imperfect grasp of the underlying purpose of an element or unit. This extra evidence may serve no useful purpose and may waste the time of whoever is assessing your portfolio. To avoid this, go systematically through your evidence, beginning *after* the introductory section checking *each piece* of evidence by asking yourself the following questions:

- is this evidence relevant to the unit(s) and if so, to which element(s)?
- does the evidence demonstrate competent performance, have I explained the context in which the tasks are done, or does it demonstrate underpinning knowledge or understanding?
- is the evidence recent and authentic, in other words, does it prove that I am currently competent?
- does the evidence refer to one or more elements and performance criteria, and if so, which?

If there is doubt about any items, put these to one side and/or get advice.

Sufficiency

Check that there is sufficient evidence. You will recall that there needs to be proof that you can competently perform any tasks required on a number of occasions, ie, sufficiency of evidence. Sometimes there will be guidance on this in the materials supplied with the standards pack: otherwise, evidence that tasks have been competently performed to standards on three separate occasions should suffice. There should also be as much performance evidence covering the required range as possible.

Validity

The next task is to sort the evidence out according to your chosen system, and check it off against the elements and performance criteria within the award to ensure that all of these have been covered and that your evidence is proof of the competences you are claiming. For this, you really need some form of list. This checklist will also help you to cross-reference items of evidence.

Evidence checklist for: D32/33								
Pg	Evidence	321	322	323	324	331	332	333
	assessment for 3 candidates	a-f	a-d			a-f		
	work placement agreement	a,b, d						
	observation checklists, feedback comments, observation notes		a-f		a-c	a-f	a-f	
	project & criteria for assessment			a-f				
	assignment feedback forms				a-d			a-e, g
	lists of questions for 3 elements		a.b e					
	audiotape- assessing 2 candidates	o	ab ce					
	APL portfolio						a-f	
	internal assessment records				a,d e			
	copy of awarding body assessment record				ad ef			def

Figure 10.3 *Example of an evidence checklist for D32/33*

Linking evidence to performance criteria

At this point you need to label the evidence according to the element(s), performance criteria and range represented. The way that your evidence is arranged will influence the way in which you choose to do this. The list below shows how a sample of evidence (eg, GNVQ) could be indexed for D33:

- an assignment contract drawn up between the candidate assessor and the student, stating the intended outcomes of the assignment, the nature of the evidence to be presented, and the method and time-scale of assessment (D331 a–f, and range–young adult)
- the student's written assignment, (D322 a, and range–project)
- the assignment marking scheme completed by the candidate assessor (D332 b,c)
- a note to the student's personal tutor asking for comments on the assignment, with reply (D332 d,e,f and range – judgement of other assessors)
- written feedback to the student from the candidate assessor, which includes questions relating to inconsistencies in the evidence (D332 e, D333 a–d)

Evidence Statements

Standards Reference: Element Reference: D323

Evidence Statements

Performance   Portfolio Ref.
Criteria Ref.

a)   Written and oral questions are selected to infer competence   #015A
     across the range based on agreed assessment plan. See   #016
     C & G written test 726-420-A1 for candidate #012 and   #008G2
     written answers to multi-choice questions for Maria &
     William

b)   The questions are based on potential performance and are   #015A
     clear, justifiable and not leading. Each question has an   #007
     objective reference in the Log Book.

c)   The inference of competence is based on a 70% minimum   #015A
     achievement by the candidate as stated in the candidate's   #015B
     instructions (see written test).

d)   All present tests are administered according to the specifications   #012A
     of the awarding body (see item 2.2 of Evidence Sheet 4b).
     See preset C&G Exam 7261-401-01/04 and 9AS 2498/02,   #017
     Page 9.   #018B,E,F

e)   The questions used were clear and not leading. This allowed   #008A1
     the candidates to explain their reasoning and to be drawn out #005A1
     on their understanding & knowledge using open questions   #008C
     (eg. GWH)

f)   Maximum access is arranged for candidates with special needs.
     All modules and elements of the course are learner-led and any   #012C
     difficulties/needs are identified early in the learning process.

Claimed (Date):   13/4/94   Signed: ..*Rory Barrett* Candidate

                      Claim Supported by: J.TUCKER.... (TDA-Print Name)

                               Signed: J.M.Tucker... TDA

Figure 10.4 *Examples of indexed and cross-referenced material for a D32 assessment*

- a self-assessment sheet, completed by the student (D332 d,e,f and range – candidate report)
- completed course documentation, with date passed to course leader (D333 e,f and range – records of assessment decisions and evidence, confident candidate, with evidence sufficient to make a decision).

Seven pieces of evidence are included here for the unit, covering all elements but not the whole of the performance criteria or range. Other evidence would need to be presented to demonstrate that the candidate was competent in the missing areas.

Figure 10.4 gives examples of collections of evidence made by candidate assessors. All the materials and documentation related to the assessment are kept together in a wallet. Each *individual* piece of evidence is marked with the relevant element, performance criteria and range, and the front of the wallet has a comprehensive listing of all the contents.

Make a final overall check to ensure that there is sufficiency of evidence, particularly across the range. Any evidence gaps *must* be met by the provision of appropriate evidence, whether through documentation, direct observation, witness testimonies, or any other suitable method. Once you are certain that sufficient evidence can be provided to cover the requirements, double-check the order in which the evidence will be presented and give each piece a reference number or letter. Any sequential system, whether numeric or alphabetical will suffice. This now enables you to draw up a list of contents or index, with 'page' numbers. You may have decided that some proofs of competence will be provided by showing the assessor work-based materials or practices, but you can still indicate in the portfolio where the evidence can be found, ie, *how* you are claiming competence.

Putting the evidence in context

Using storyboards

Although it is probably obvious to *you*, an assessor may find it difficult to understand or interpret the evidence presented. Therefore, there must be some explanation as to the context in which you acquired your evidence. As mentioned before, there is no reason why this cannot be done orally, but if the majority of your evidence is being presented in a portfolio it may save assessor time to either write an explanatory statement about the evidence for each element, and attach it to the relevant work, or to complete a storyboard, which is a logical description of how and why the evidence for a particular element demonstrates your competence. Some awarding bodies, eg, IPD, include storyboards as part of their documentation.

The statements and storyboards, used in conjunction with a clear list of the evidence included, should make the portfolio self-explanatory. Indeed, your aim should be to get the portfolio to the point at which it can be happily

STORYBOARD

Comments on evidence collection   D323

Evidence for this element was based on the specifications for competence laid down by City & Guilds and the Training Authority.

The written and oral questions are based on objective references in Log Books, maintained by each learner. When candidates understand the contents of each log book, they are agreed before the tests and the performance criteria are adhered to in inferring competent performance.

Assessment takes place only when the candidate is ready. During my course, candidates sit 3 City & Guilds Exams. Two of these require candidates to sit written as well as practical tests.

All tests take place in the training room and are closely and strictly supervised.

Figure 10.5 *A sample storyboard*

handed to an assessor who has no knowledge of your work, feeling that nothing would have to be verbally explained.

Completing official documentation

It is imperative that you complete any documentation supplied by the awarding body. (You may already have used some of this in completing the abovementioned tasks.) There are usually two types of form, one which details the evidence supplied for each element, to be signed by the assessor and the candidate, and one which is a final record of achievement, to be signed by the assessor, the candidate and both the internal and external verifiers. Some forms ask you to separate out your evidence into APL, direct and supplementary categories. Ensure that you have signed and dated wherever required on the documentation, otherwise the certification process may be delayed.

A final word

Remember that the portfolio is merely a means for you to demonstrate your competence through the presentation of evidence to the assessor for final assessment. Its format will depend on the nature of your evidence – it may be heavily paper-based if a lot of evidence is from APL, but if the majority of the evidence is from recent performance, there may be a greater emphasis on observations of practice and/or taped evidence. Again, you may have met much of the knowledge and understanding required through your performance or APL evidence, or you may have completed some assignments or questionnaires. Everybody's portfolio will be, and should be, different. The important thing is that you have analysed and thought about the way in which you assess, and used this as an opportunity to improve or reduce any gaps in your own assessment performance.

Summary

This chapter should have helped you:

- decide on a sensible method for evidence presentation
- organize and check your evidence against performance criteria, range statements and supplementary evidence
- index and cross-reference the evidence
- write storyboards and evidence statements
- complete the required documentation.

11 Assessing your Evidence

Your assessment plan; methods of portfolio assessment; the assessment interview; assessment at a distance; internal verification; external verification; certification.

This chapter covers the practicalities of the final assessment for an award from the candidate's point of view; the methods described here can also be used as a model for assessing any competence-based award.

Your assessment plan

Just as you should be used to creating and agreeing assessment plans with your own trainees, it follows that you should have an agreed plan for your own assessment, which has been drawn up by yourself, your adviser (if you have one) and the assessor, and agreed by all the involved parties. Check that all the details are clear to you, and that you have all the information that you need. (Sample assessment plans can also be found in Chapter 9.)

When you are ready for assessment, it is important that you, the candidate, are clear on the verification and certification procedures, and are reminded of any associated costs at this time, particularly if there is an hourly, instead of a flat rate for assessment. In other words, the assessment process you undertake as a candidate yourself should, like the assessment processes used with your own candidates, hold no surprises. Many centres give pre-assessment portfolio checks, which include thorough examination of your evidence against the performance criteria, range statements and required supplementary evidence.

Methods of portfolio assessment

This is often a matter of personal choice with assessors, and can range from an informal chat between assessor and candidate which leads into formal assessment, to a structured interview based around questions the assessor has determined. Some assessors like to have the portfolio in advance of the interview, in order to help the selection of appropriate questions. The important thing to remember is that *it is up to you as the candidate* to demonstrate competence against the standards; it is *not* the assessors' function to help you to do this. Assessors are just as likely to ignore evidence which is unclear to them as they are to ask for clarification. If you have a choice of assessment locations, it is probably worth considering whether it would be more advantageous to be assessed at your workplace, in case you are required to provide additional evidence. This may be easily available in workplace files or from colleagues, and will avoid the need for reassessment at a later date.

ASSESSMENT PLAN

TDLB UNITS

NAME: *Jill Hancock*

PROGRAMME: *Trainer's Award*

ORGANIZATION: *Grayford Training*

DETAILS OF UNITS AND ELEMENTS TO BE ASSESSED:

D32 Elements

TIME, DATE AND PLACE OF ASSESSMENT:

930-1130 am. Wed. 13th April 1994. Grayford Training - Training Room T5

TIME, DATE AND PLACE OF FEEDBACK:

10 am. Friday 15th April 1994. Grayford Training - Room 4B

EVIDENCE:

Portfolio of evidence to cover D32
-   observation checklists completed
-   answers to verbal questions from assessor

NB filing cabinets will need to be accessed for evidence

ACTION TO BE TAKEN BEFORE ASSESSMENT:

Assessment Plan Discussed and Agreed

Signature of Candidate: Signature of Assessor:

Figure 11.1 *An assessment plan for an assessor award*

The assessment interview

Irrespective of your position and experience, an assessment interview can still be a stressful occasion, if only because you may be highly practised and knowledgeable, and that you will be *expecting* to be deemed competent! The assessor may ask you to describe or explain your evidence, so use the portfolio itself to save time, and remember that the assessor just may have missed something which you know is included. Usually, the interview will focus on the checking of performance criteria and range statements for which there is apparently no evidence, and in checking out underpinning knowledge and understanding. The assessor should have a pre-prepared list of questions, from which an appropriate selection is made in true D32/33 style. See Chapter 3 for help on devising questions to check underpinning knowledge and

1. How had this assessment been agreed with your candidate?
2. What determined the physical arrangements, eg, where you stood, when you asked questions?
3. What did you do to encourage the candidate to select and present relevant evidence?
4. How did you decide/construct the questions you asked orally? Are the questions written down?
5. What is your definition of a 'leading question'? How can you avoid asking them?
6. Why did you ask the number of questions that you did?
7. How are you sure that you can infer competent performance in other situations where the task/activity might occur?
8. In what ways can you involve candidates in their own assessments? How effective was the candidates' performance in this case? How might it be improved?
9. What rules do you follow when giving feedback?
10. How do you encourage individuals to ask questions as a natural part of the feedback and evaluation process?
11. What makes this assessment fair, reliable, valid and sufficient?
12. Did this candidate have any special needs for which you had to cater? What special needs might candidates have and how would you accommodate these?
13. Are there any aspects of my assessment of you about which you are unclear, or which you wish to discuss further?

Figure 11.2 *A sample of questions for use with assessment observations*

understanding, which are likely to be similar to the questions your assessor might ask you. Figure 11.2 gives a sample list of questions for use during a D32 assessment of natural performance which you might be asked during any part of the interview which relates to observation of performance.

If you have had the opportunity to work through similar lists of questions beforehand (for assessment techniques and for underpinning knowledge and understanding), you could include your answers as supplementary evidence, as it may save unnecessary oral questioning. On the other hand, you may prefer to prepare the answers mentally, and answer oral questions rather than put a lot down in writing. The assessor will also be determining the authenticity of your evidence – this is particularly important where candidates have been working as part of a team and where there may be some 'common' evidence. If this is the case, it is really important that candidates are clear about why the evidence demonstrates *their* competence, rather than that of a team itself or of another team member.

You should of course receive constructive feedback after the assessment. Some assessors will give this verbally, but usually there will be a short written report confirming satisfaction with the evidence, or detailing where competence has not been fully shown.

Assessments can vary considerably in time. We have known assessments vary between 30 minutes and two and a half hours for the assessment of APL portfolios for D32/33. The variation has been due to the *amount* of evidence presented, the *nature* of the evidence (one assessor insisted on watching the whole of an assessment recorded on video, which was additional to written performance evidence), the overall grasp of the assessment process shown by the candidate, and the candidate's ability to respond concisely to the details needed. 'New' assessors frequently take longer to complete the assessment process due to a variety of factors, not least of which can be the lack of coordinated planning of assessment opportunities in the workplace and the impulse to request additional material to 'be on the safe side'.

Assessment at a distance

This is uncommon, but is possible, provided the process has been agreed with the verifiers concerned. The portfolio needs to be exemplary in nature, since the assessor will need to gain all information from a private examination, and will definitely need to contain both a description of the process undergone to gather evidence and evidence of underpinning knowledge and understanding. Even so, it is highly likely that the assessor will want to talk to the candidate on the telephone in order to satisfy themselves as to the authenticity of the evidence provided.

Case study: European candidates

As a result of a TEC-funded project, four candidates from Eire decided to see if the TDLB standards transferred to their workplace settings. Since NVQs were not adopted in the Republic, all set about devising (or adapting from syllabi) their own 'elements and performance criteria'. In some cases, particularly for one candidate working for the Irish Training Authority, the procedures being followed were very similar to those required for internal verification. The candidates were assessed in the workplace by an accredited assessor. They then received telephone support and guidance from this assessor who now acted as an adviser, and because they had opted for an awarding body which favoured personal development and reflection, then spent some time building up their portfolios before final assessment. The portfolios were sent to the accredited centre in England for internal verification.

You need to consider the associated costs of sending portfolios to the assessor. If you use a courier parcel service there may be costs of around £50. Another candidate who was assessed at a distance had a few uneasy nights when part of their portfolio became mislaid *in* the assessment centre to which it had been sent!

Internal verification

After the portfolio has been successfully assessed, it may need to be sampled by the assessment centre's internal verifier. On no account should this person be the same as the one who assessed the portfolio. If this appears to be the case, you should make enquiries, and if found to be true, consider reporting the centre, as their practice would be against the Awarding Bodies Common Accord (see Chapter 4), an important document which is intended to improve the quality of the assessment system. It may be some time before the internal verification process is completed, as portfolios have to be sampled, assessor practice monitored, and documentation completed. Your assessment plan may give some indication of the time-scale involved. It is possible that the internal verifier may wish to speak to you about the assessment process you have undergone, and could ask to be present while you are being assessed. If this is the case, it should have been agreed with you. The internal verifier will need to sign relevant documentation in your portfolio and provide a report to the external verifier about the assessment process undertaken by candidates.

External verification

The role of the external verifier is explained in Chapters 2 and 4. Each centre will have one or more external verifiers depending on the range of awards that are offered. Centres approved to offer the assessor/verifier/APL adviser awards are usually entitled to three visits by the external verifier per year, although a centre can request additional visits. Any additional visits have to be approved by the awarding body and have to be paid for separately by the centre. If you are in a particular hurry to have the assessment process fully complete, and there would be a delay of some months before the routine visit of the external verifier, it might be worthwhile to find out from the centre if an additional visit could be arranged, bearing in mind that you will no doubt have to pay for this! If the centre is still under provisional approval, the external verifier will need to look at every portfolio but if the centre has full approval, sampling is undertaken on a percentage or other statistical basis; either way, it is likely that you will have to either resubmit your portfolio at the appropriate time or leave it at the centre after assessment.

Certification

Your completed record of achievement should be returned to you after external verification. The relevant administrative staff at the centre will submit the required documentation to the awarding body. You will have provided information such as your date of birth and the name which you wish to have printed on the certificate when you register (which always precedes the formal assessment process). If you have previously registered with a particular awarding body for another qualification, you may need to supply the registration number to the centre, since some awarding bodies now give candidates a 'unique' number for life. The time taken between a centre applying for certification and the receipt of certificates can range from a few weeks to several months, although the latter is unusual. The centre will not be able to send off any documentation until after the external verification visit, so bear this in mind when calculating the expected date of arrival of your certificate. Clarify with the centre what happens once they receive the certificate – some centres post them to candidates and others prefer you to call, for security reasons.

Summary

This chapter should have helped you:

- prepare for evidence assessment
- prepare for portfolio assessment
- know what happens in internal verification of your evidence
- understand how external verification and certification will be undertaken.

12 Conclusion

Embedding the process

It is a sad, if understandable, fact that many who embark on the process of evidence collection for assessing and verifying do so reluctantly and sometimes cynically. Often, candidates for the awards have been operating in the field for many years and may be very good at their jobs; they may have been approved to assess vocational competence by an awarding body and find it difficult to understand why they must jump through yet 'another hoop', in the guise of TDLB awards. They are probably extremely busy and are unlikely to be given any time by their organizations in which to collect, let along *present*, evidence of competence; they may have taken several similar awards within the past few years, and see TDLB awards as just another government initiative, soon to be superseded by something else. Whatever the reasons, and however valid they may be, the fact remains that what has to be done has to be done, and the task is likely to be less onerous if the candidate can see some personal benefit in addition to acquiring a certificate. Almost without exception, even the grumpiest and most recalcitrant candidates we have been involved with, have, in the end, grudgingly conceded that some or all of the following have happened as a result of undertaking the exercise:

- their practice can be demonstrated to be fair, reliable and consistent
- useful documentation has been produced enabling candidates and staff to keep track of assessments and feedback
- practice within a section has been standardized
- they have been able to reappraise practice
- they have had to examine and sometimes update knowledge of assessment procedures
- assessments have been made more efficient due to the use of a wider range of techniques
- record-keeping has improved, helping with the monitoring of successful outcomes.

There are no doubt other benefits which have occurred, and of which we are unaware, and it is true to say that for some organizations and individuals, the pain has been at least as great as the gain. However, we are convinced of the value of the assessment of competence against standards, *providing that assessors and candidates are able to reflect upon the process, and providing that the acquisition of relevant knowledge and understanding goes alongside the collection of performance evidence*. If this does not happen, any value in the activity is likely to be lost and, more importantly, it is unlikely that the standards will be maintained.

Using the standards for development

Equally important is the need to *maintain a developmental rather than a mechanistic approach to competence,* in other words, to use the standards in a holistic, questioning and creative way rather than solely as a prescriptive, narrow and fragmented way of assessing competence outcomes. This often needs addressing by organizations using standards as much as by individuals. When the standards were first published by TDLB in 1992, the potential benefits of an imaginative approach to their use was given in the Executive Summary, namely:

- as a basis for job descriptions
- to identify training needs
- to develop training programmes
- as a basis for assessment
- as benchmarks for development
- to form vocational qualifications.

The Summary also stated the expectation that the National Standards for Training and Development would 'enable employers to design, promote and support the kinds of personal and professional development cultures they needed to create and sustain amongst their workforces' by:

- providing basic requirement specifications that could be used in the purchase of training services
- indicating the kinds of criteria that should be used to evaluate the progress and outcomes of training programmes
- acting as an operational guide to the design, development and delivery of training programmes
- underpinning the introduction and use of innovative, non-traditional training methods, systems and materials
- incorporating best practice in human resource development planning and strategy design approaches
- providing ways of reaping the obvious benefits of workplace assessment to specific standards by qualified assessors and verifiers.

One of the biggest problems faced by individual candidates and by organizations which are supporting their staff to acquire relevant awards, is that of discovering that either job roles are narrower than the standards require, or that practices and procedures do not tally with the standards requirements. While sensitive and informed advice can help candidates to choose appropriate standards to demonstrate competence, the discovery can lead to resentment of a competence-based approach to outcomes measurement and create problems with trust and motivation. This can be a particular problem where there are difficulties in agreeing on the interpretation of standards, where staff feel threatened (eg, does lack of demonstrated competence equal *in*competence?), and where tried and tested procedures are being changed to accommodate the new approaches. Where organizational practice is concerned, it is not uncommon to find that a complete programme of staff development takes place, sometimes deriving from the discovery that assessment practices across departments differ significantly. The standards can also be used successfully to give a fair framework to traditional, process-based programmes and, in particular, discussion related to implementation of standards can, in itself, be a powerful tool for staff development as current job roles, programme content and assessment techniques are compared with those that would be required.

Maintaining and improving quality

The verification roles are designed to uphold the continuous implementation of the standards. Internal verifiers are the key to continuous quality improvement as they will gain an overview of practice and lead the assessment team towards a sharing of good practice. Practices and procedures introduced into one section of an organization due to the implementation of a standards-based programme can be the catalyst for adoption by another section. Likewise, there may be opportunities for rationalizing paperwork or moving towards a function-based rather than programme-based approach to student/trainee needs analysis, delivery and assessment, which in turn may improve the efficiency and effectiveness of monitoring candidate throughput.

Objections to NVQs

Some of those involved with education and training find it particularly hard to accept that NVQs are not concerned with how someone *learned* to do something, or what training they received, but are only concerned with whether someone can perform a job of work to a required standard. This assessment-driven model has produced the same kind of arguments as those related to the National Curriculum, ie, that too much time is being spent on testing at the expense of learning. We feel that this concern is based on a misunderstanding of the nature of NVQs. It is important to emphasize again that NVQs are a means of *accrediting* learning or experience, unlike qualifications such as 'A' levels or GCSEs which are closely linked to formal programmes of learning. So whereas these concerns are relevant to educational programmes where the 'learning' time allocated to a course of study is being taken up with tests, we do not believe that they are relevant to NVQs where learning and assessment are divorced. As an illustration of this, an individual could have done the same type of work for five years. During that time they will have learned a great deal. Maybe they will have been on a course to improve their skills and knowledge, yet they will have no formal qualifications to recognize what they can do, ie, the *practical end product* of learning or experience. The important factor will not be how or when the learning took place, but how competently that individual can now perform. NVQs merely provide accreditation of that confidence.

There are, however, a number of significant objections to NVQs which could affect their ability to be adopted nationally at all levels. There are doubts about the process of functional analysis by which the standards have been developed. A particular concern is that this process provides too narrow and mechanical a framework to analyse jobs which are complex in nature, or to deal with work that involves professional ethics and values. Another major issue is that NVQs are not concerned with how much knowledge someone has about a particular area, only how far that knowledge informs their ability to perform a particular job of work competently. This raises questions about the nature of knowledge and whether occupational areas have a 'body' of knowledge which should provide an overall context for the skills required, and which cannot operate in this fashion if separated into discrete areas and linked closely with specific competences. Indeed, the issue of 'competence' in general has produced an energetic and passionate debate, with opponents of NVQs criticizing them for supporting a mechanistic approach that leaves no room for identification of excellence, and that encourages mediocrity rather than high performance. It is evident that if the new qualifications system is to be accepted and adopted on a large scale, these concerns should not be perceived as irrelevant but need to be addressed thoroughly and convincingly by NCVQ and the awarding bodies.

A recent report on education (Smithers, 1993) highlighted a range of real and perceived problems with the assessment of NVQs and GNVQs. To respond adequately to all the points made in the report is beyond the scope of this book, but if the research is accurate, it appears that there are candidates who are having their work assessed solely by those that have trained them (not illegal, but undesirable), and who are being assessed in a limited way, often *only* on the basis of observation and simple questioning techniques. The assessment process as defined in the standards is, as we have seen, comprehensive. Assessors should be assessing using a *range* of techniques particularly at level 3 and above. They need not be limited by the documentation provided by a Lead Body, nor by the performance criteria. True, knowledge and understanding are *inferred* by the competent performance of a task, but an assessor assessing to D32/33 standards *must* check for the knowledge and understanding required, at least by the administration of pre-set, oral, written and assessor-devised questions as appropriate. Programme design is, quite simply, left to the professional judgement of trainers and assessors. While external verifiers are mainly systems and procedures monitors, they can also be instrumental in the exploration and development of ideas through the sharing of their experiences gained at national and regional level.

Finally

We believe that the revised standards for assessment, verification and advising provide a good framework from which to work in a constructive way with candidates on competence-based programmes. However, unless there is adequate funding to enable proper support of programmes, unless there is a requirement for qualifications, underpinned by policies which provide work instead of work experience, in an environment where there is at least a semblance of stability, it is unlikely that there will be any significant improvement in the quality of Britain's workforce, despite an improved and appropriate system for assessment of competence.

Case Studies – Sample Portfolios of Evidence

1. A beauty therapist assessing NVQs in her own salon: evidence for D32

- contents page
- description of her work and how she assesses
- rough notes made on discussion with candidate about what she was going to be assessed on. Date and time for assessment agreed and noted. Notes signed by candidate as a genuine record of discussion
- information sheet for trainees prepared by salon owner giving details of NVQ assessment
- C&G assessment guidelines
- C&G assessment schedule booklet
- examples of oral questions used during and after observation of a candidate carrying out a manicure. Ticked for correct answers
- checklist completed by internal verifier covering a number of performance criteria observed to be demonstrated by the salon owner while she was assessing three different candidates
- certificate of attendance at an NVQ workshop on NVQ level 2 in beauty therapy
- assessment sheets completed by the salon owner during observation of two candidates carrying out facial massage and manicure
- client record card with details of treatments and candidate's comments
- written records of feedback given to three different candidates with space for candidates to record their comments; comments highlighted where appropriate, eg, one candidate said she felt really relaxed because of the way the assessment had been handled
- three completed record sheets showing what units and elements had been achieved by candidates
- signed statement from internal verifier that she received all necessary records within the time-scale allowed.

The salon owner wrote explanatory statements where necessary. She was also questioned on a number of areas during the assessment interview.

2. An assessor of NVQ business administration: evidence for D33

- contents page
- certificate of attendance at an NVQ conference
- sample of literature from NVQ with highlighted areas of relevance

- minutes of meeting between tutors and assessors about NVQs
- copies from trainees' work diaries
- simulation chart showing administrative and organizational details of simulations used for assessment
- samples of tasks carried out through simulation
- four samples of assignments
- certification record
- witness statements from candidates
- candidate achievement matrix
- copy of assessment programme for candidate
- feedback sheets.

3. A designated internal verifier (IV) for an accredited centre: evidence for D34

- contents page
- vocational qualification certificates and D32/33 certificate
- notes on key issues for the centre relating to internal verification
- programme of an assessor/verifier support network meeting at which the IV candidate was giving a presentation; minutes of previous meeting to show attendance; memo showing distribution of this material to in-house assessors
- list of materials received from awarding body (on disk, updated)
- allocation plan of assessment arrangements
- records made by assessors (in filing cabinet)
- notes of a meeting (observed by external verifier) between IV candidate and two assessors, one experienced and one relatively new; observation notes show that advice was given regarding the collection and judgement of evidence
- records of training opportunities for assessors; requests from assessors for information and guidance; review sheets used with assessors; notes of training undertaken by assessors
- minutes of meetings between assessors and IV candidate showing the occurrence of meetings where all assessors have been involved in judging the same evidence
- dated notes referring to the monitoring of candidate records (in filing cabinet) in relation to four elements of competence for three candidates
- notes relating to a submission for certification and associated documentation in respect of one candidate (administrative staff section, filing cabinet)
- a specification of internal verification and assessment procedures
- submission to awarding body, assessor CVs and copies of D32/33 certificates (in filing cabinet)
- records of conducting internal verification in relation to three assessment decisions.

4. An adviser-candidate for APL – construction specialist: evidence for D36

- contents page
- vocational qualification certificates
- certificate from CITB approving adviser-candidate as an assessor
- full details of NVQs in carpentry and joinery and decorative trades, well-used and annotated
- register of candidates for interview and advice
- informal notes made during interviews with two candidates
- witness statements from two candidates
- letter of validation from counselling and guidance unit manager
- completed reviews for two candidates (each covering three elements of competence)
- observation checklist completed by an assessor of an interview with a candidate to agree an action plan
- records of advice and assistance for one candidate (covering three elements of competence)
- photocopy of candidate's NVQ unit at level 2 in carpentry and joinery, gained by them through APL.

Glossary of Terms

All terms are commonly used in training; there is an emphasis on terms related to assessment.

Access (to assessment) making sure that candidates can be assessed in the most appropriate ways; ensuring that barriers to assessment are minimized; enabling candidates to have some control over the assessment process.

Accreditation the formal recognition of a candidates' work against prescribed criteria; candidates can be accredited for all or part of a unit, or in all or part of an award.

Accreditation centre *see* Centre. Also AAC, ADAC (pg 64).

Accreditation of Prior Learning (APL) the formal recognition of work done previously, which is eligible to count towards an award; this work can be from both certificated sources, eg, qualifications, and uncertificated sources, eg, from previous experience (also: APEL Accreditation of Prior Experimental Learning; APA Accreditation of Prior Achievment).

Achievement the amount of skill, knowledge or understanding which an individual is able to demonstrate; standards of achievement are used in GNVQs rather than standards of competence.

Action plans the tasks an individual needs to undertake to reach particular goals; plans usually include target and review dates, and are often agreed with a supervisor; they may cover any time period, one or more goals, and may be recorded on formal documentation or be in note form.

Assessment (competence-based) judging the degree to which a candidate has met predetermined criteria; candidates must show that they can do certain tasks in a prescribed way and that they know the context of the task and why it must be performed in certain ways.

Assessment centre *see* Centre.

Assessment criteria the standards against which assessments are judged: they must be explicit before the assessment is agreed and undertaken; they determine the minimum of what must be taught, if part of a programme of learning.

Assessment instruments these are not some medieval torture device, but the range of questionnaires, tests, checklists and other materials used to assess specific skills, knowledge, qualities, or understanding; for example, there are tests designed to pick out weaknesses in grammar, or count the number of facts remembered, or tell us how confident we are; languages can be tested through the use of specially designed audiotapes, and skills by using real or simulated work tasks.

Assessment opportunities the range of options to candidate and assessor to determine competence or achievement; these may be work-based, or training centre/college-based; they may be formally planned, occur during normal work, and be based on a whole range of sources of evidence; candidates and assessors need to be aware that there may be alternative opportunities to assessment from those normally used.

Assessment plans an agreed statement between candidate and assessor, normally written, of how the candidate will demonstrate competence; plans may cover whole or part awards, and whole or part units; assessment plans need to specify as a minimum what will be assessed, the criteria for assessment, how the assessment will be undertaken and by whom, the time-scale involved and any special arrangements that need to be made: assessment plans can be for individuals or for groups.

Assessor-devised questions questions composed by the assessor as opposed to being drawn from a bank of prepared questions produced by, for example, an awarding body.

Assignments practical or written tasks given to candidates which test skills, knowledge or understanding, or combinations of all three; tasks should be explicit and candidates should be clear about what is required of them.

Authentic evidence can be established as being that of the candidate rather than that of another, or of a group; if group work is used as evidence, the candidate's contribution should be clearly identifiable.

Award a certificate or record of achievement issued by an awarding body which confirms accreditation; in the case of the 'Assessor Awards', 'Verifier Awards' and the 'APL Award', the awarding bodies have identified one or more units from the TDLB standards and offered them as a 'package'; some of the awards consist of units which form part of a full NVQ.

Awarding body a body (organization) which gives awards, eg, BTEC, Royal Society of Arts, Construction Industry Training Board; all awarding bodies which give NVQs (including the assessor and verifier awards) must first be approved by the NCVQ.

Barriers (to access) anything (physical or mental) which prevents a candidate from taking up opportunities for training or assessment.

Candidate a person who is preparing to be assessed for an award; in this book, the term is used to indicate anyone who is presenting themselves for assessment, eg, someone being assessed for NVQs within the workplace, or someone being assessed for GNVQs in a school; depending on the context, the candidate can be an employee/client/trainee/student/pupil.

Candidate-(student-) centred any approach in training and assessment which considers the needs of the candidate, and which involves the candidate in making choices about the processes to be used.

Candidate reports used in range statements to indicate oral or written reports from the candidate which involve descriptions of activities and processes and some self-assessment, eg, a work diary.

Centre an organization approved by an awarding body to assess and accredit on its behalf; its advisers, assessors and internal verifiers should also all be approved by the awarding body.

Certification the process of registration, assessment, recording results, completing documentation, applying for and receiving certificates.

Competence the ability to perform within a work-related function or occupational area to national standards expected in employment.

Contingencies the unexpected occurrences that can happen at work and that a candidate will need to show that they can deal with; a candidate's competence in dealing with contingencies is often explored through use of questioning, eg 'what if...?' questions; simulations may be another means by which the candidate can be assessed.

Continuous assessment making judgements on a candidate's performance or ability over a period of time.

Core skills a set of generic skills, transferable across all occupational areas; they are incorporated into all GNVQ programmes, with mandatory units on communications, application of numbers and information technology, and optional units on personal skills (working with others, and improving our own learning and performance), and problem-solving.

Credit accumulation an arrangement which enables candidates to collect individual units or elements of competence over a period of time; these can then be matched and accredited against appropriate awards or qualifications; reassessment does not have to take place should a credit be used for credit transfer; many Credit Accumulation and Transfer Schemes (CATS) already exist in higher education and in future will be in further education as well.

Credit transfer using credits (units, qualifications) from one award to count towards another different (but usually related) award.

Criterion-referenced judgements made against agreed criteria.

Currency refers to evidence which shows the candidate can competently perform at the time of the assessment; currency often depends on the subject, eg, computing changes quickly, bricklaying techniques less swiftly; evidence less than two years old is usually required – all cases need to be individually negotiated.

Curriculum all the aspects of learning, including methods, resources and syllabus content that make up a programme of study.

Direct assessment assessing a product or process, eg, a cake, a completed stocksheet, a training session.

Differing sources of evidence see diverse evidence.

Direct evidence evidence which the candidate has produced themself.

Direct support help is offered directly to the candidate, eg, offering advice.

Diverse evidence evidence drawn from a number of different sources, including natural performance; see range for D33.

Element (of competence) a description of a single action, behaviour or outcome required to be demonstrated separately; a number of elements make up each unit; for assessment purposes, elements can be accredited separately; all elements must have been accredited before a unit award is given.

Evaluation judging the value of something through gathering data from a variety of sources, eg, interviews, questionnaires, informal discussions, results, and analysing this feedback.

Evidence information from a variety of sources which proves a candidate's competence; the word is occasionally used as a verb, when it refers to the process of logging relevant activities as evidence.

Experiential learning learning which has happened through and from experience, as opposed to formal programmes of education or training; much adult learning occurs in this way, and the learner often needs help to recognize skills, knowledge and understanding gained in non-formal ways.

External assessment assessment by an assessor who is not part of (is external to) the assessment or accreditation centre.

External verifier a person appointed by the awarding body who approves assessment centres and then regularly monitors their operation to national standards; they act as a quality assurance link between the approved centre and the awarding body.

Fairness ensuring just and equitable conditions in the assessment process for all candidates, eg, by providing for candidates with special assessment needs, and by following the national standards for assessment.

Feedback reviewing a process and giving constructive oral or written comment to the candidate so that they understand the strengths and weaknesses of their performance/evidence and understand what to do as a consequence.

Formative assessment assessment made to help determine future actions and development, or to confirm progress.

Functional analysis the process of breaking down a whole job or task into its component pieces according to the different tasks performed in that job; NVQ competences have been determined through the process of functional analysis.

Generic competences competences which occur across many occupational areas, eg, competence in maintaining standards of safety, competence in working with people; competence in assessment is a generic competence, as individuals have to be able to assess as part of their job role within every occupational area.

General National Vocational Qualification a vocationally-related qualification covering a broad based occupational area and aimed primarily at 16–19-year-olds in full-time education.

Indirect support help for the candidate is organized from another source, eg, by putting them in touch with someone who could train them in certain techniques.

Industry Lead Body (ILB) a group representing a particular industry or employment sector and which specifies the standards of competence required for employment within that sector; sometimes known as Lead Industry Bodies.

Internal assessment assessment by an assessor who is a member of staff of the assessment or accreditation centre with which the candidate is registered.

Internal verifier a person approved by the external verifier to coordinate the assessment processes and practices within a centre, and who liaises with the external verifier and the awarding bodies.

Knowledge evidence a means of showing that a candidate knows and understands both what they are doing and the context in which they are working; knowledge evidence is also a means of showing that the candidate knows what to do in a range of different situations.

Level (of qualification) NVQs have five levels from basic competence (level 1) to strategic management (level 5); the levels are determined by job role and are defined on the basis of the skill, knowledge and understanding required, together with the degree of responsibility and supervision involved in performing the related work roles.

Lead Industry Body (LIB) *see* ILB.

Log book a document issued by many awarding bodies to candidates in which detailed tasks and tests are set out together with the required units and elements of competence; both assessor and candidate are required to sign in the books as competence is confirmed.

Moderation a process whereby the results of assessments from more than one source are compared together and against an agreed, accepted, standard; moderation can be internally or externally conducted.

Moderator a person (approved by an awarding body if an external moderator) to conduct moderation, usually with considerable experience in the curriculum area; they often help with training and with interpretation of the curriculum.

Module a self-contained unit of learning which can build towards a qualification; a BTEC leisure studies course might include modules in organizing sporting events and obtaining sponsorship for sport.

National Council for Vocational Qualifications the body which approves NCVQs and which monitors the system.

National Vocational Qualification a qualification related to employment, recognized by the NVQ, and part of an approved framework of levels; an NVQ is *not* a course; NVQs are awarded when a candidate has successfully demonstrated competence in a number of units of competence related to job role.

Natural performance the way in which a candidate normally undertakes tasks in the course of their employment.

Naturally occurring evidence evidence which occurs as a normal part of an individual's work, ie, part of their job or part of a programme of study.

Norm-referenced assessment assessment which is judged against the achievements of others undertaking the same assessment; grades awarded depend on the ability not only of the candidate/student, but of the whole group under consideration.

Occupational standards set by ILBs, these are standards which have usually been derived by a process of functional analysis; the standards are set for each element of a task within a complete job, and cover the performance, context of operation and underpinning knowledge and understanding required.

Open access systems of learning, training, education or assessment open to as many people as possible through removing as many barriers to participation as possible.

Open learning methods of acquiring skills knowledge and understanding which do not involve traditional attendance at classes or even require contact with a tutor; they often involve the use of interactive learning packages (written or video), supplemented by appropriate tutor support.

Peer group a group of people equal in status to, or from the same or similar groups as oneself.

Peer reports oral or written descriptions of activities or processes from the candidate's peer group providing information about the candidate's performance which can be used for assessment purposes.

Performance criteria statements which indicate the standards of performance required for each element of competence; all performance criteria need to be met before an element can be accredited.

Performance evidence evidence from an activity carried out by the candidate, or something produced as a result of that activity.

Portfolio a collection of evidence, usually produced over an extended period of time, and from various sources, which is presented together as evidence of achievement; the term is sometimes used to indicate the receptacle in which the evidence is contained, eg, a ring binder.

Pre-set tests any oral or written test prepared in advance by an assessor or by an awarding body; these often form an integral part of assessment for all candidates at particular levels; they are often set out in candidate log books or are provided separately by the awarding body as in GNVQ end tests.

Prior experience experience acquired by the candidate before registering for an assessment which may provide evidence against units or elements.

Prior learning learning acquired by the candidate before registering for an assessment or training programme; this learning may or may not be certificated.

Proforma a template document devised to record a particular stage of a process or procedure.

Project an extended piece of practical and/or written work involving planning and research and often presented as a report.

Qualification a certificate legally provided which indicates that the holder has reached a necessary standard, eg, driving test certificate, an 'A' level.

Quality assurance methods by which standards are regularly checked and monitored; systems which ensure that procedures are done in certain ways, eg, BS5750 (also known as BSEN ISO 9000).

Questioning a range of techniques involving written or oral questions designed to elicit knowledge and understanding from candidates.

Range statements descriptions of the context(s) and circumstances in which performance criteria described in the element should be able to be performed by someone competent in the activity.

Record of achievement a composite record of a person's varied achievements and learning experiences over a period of time; it typically contains records of formal and informal learning experiences, credits gained, modules studied, reflections on achievements, agreed learning plans and evaluations.

Reliability the degree to which an assessment can be administered with the same results to others, the consistent ability of the assessment or the assessor to accurately distinguish between competent and non-competent performance.

Review the formal or informal process of reflecting on performance, often conducted between an adviser/assessor and a candidate, usually on a one-to-one basis; used as a basis for planning future activity.

Satellite centre an organization which conducts its own assessments under the supervision of a larger approved centre; staff follow the same practices and procedures as those of the approved centre.

Scottish Vocational Qualifications (SVQs) the Scottish equivalent of NVQs awarded by SCOTVEC.

Simulation a realistic exercise set up specifically to assess knowledge, skills or understanding; it should replicate a real work situation and should be used in circumstances where it would be difficult or costly to asses within the work context. (eg, firefighting procedure, dealing with an emergency first-aid situation). The internal verifier should be able to advise on the acceptable use of simulators.

Skill the ability to do a task or perform an activity.

Special assessment needs see special assessment requirements.

Special assessment requirements NVQs and GNVQs emphasize the importance of access to fair and reliable assessment. According to candidates' circumstances, this may involve special arrangements being made, eg, physical access.

Training needs analysis the identification of individual or organizational training needs through a systematic analysis of current skills against future performance requirements.

Transferability the ability to relate learning or performance in one area or context to another, eg, a candidate who can measure in metric in a training environment should be able to do so in the workplace using different materials and equipment.

Unit (of competence) a group of elements of competence which together constitute a particular work role, and which form the smallest grouping of competence able to be recognized separately for certification towards an award.

Underpinning (knowledge and understanding) that which ensures that tasks are not performed unthinkingly, but shows that candidates know *why* things are done in a particular way, and that they have a general and/or specific knowledge about the task overall.

Unit credit units within NVQs and GNVQs can be accredited separately; a unit is the smallest amount of achievement or competence which can be submitted to an awarding body for accreditation.

Validity an assessment process has validity if it measures what it is supposed to measure.

Verification the process of checking that the correct and agreed procedures and systems have been used.

Verifier *see* External verifier and Internal verifiers.

Work-based assessment assessments conducted in the candidate's workplace or which are made on evidence produced from or at the workplace.

Work-based learning learning which occurs at the place of work rather than, for example, through attendance on a formal programme of study based in an institution; some programmes of study do, however, include work-based learning as part of the course, eg, work experience, sandwich courses.

Work-based training training which takes place within the work environment as opposed to being conducted elsewhere.

Suggested Further Reading

Ainley, P and Corney, M (1990) *Training for the Future: The rise and fall of the MSC*, London: Cassell.

Boam, R and Sparrow, P (1992) *Designing and Achieving Competency*, Maidenhead: McGraw Hill.

BTEC (1990) *The Accreditation of Prior Learning (APL) General Guidance*, London: BTEC.

BTEC (1993) *Implementing BTEC GNVQs: A guide for centres*, London: BTEC.

CBI (1989) *Towards a Skills Revolution: Report of the vocational education and training taskforce*, London: Confederation of British Industry.

CGLI (1990) *APL Handbook: Guidance on the accreditation of prior learning*, London: City and Guilds.

Etherton, T and Houston, T (1991) *Equal Opportunities: the role of awarding bodies*, London: NCVQ.

Evans, B (1992) *The Politics of the Training Market*, London: Routledge.

FEU (1992) *TDLB Standards in Further Education*, London: Further Education Unit.

FEU (1993) *Standards in Action,* London: FEU.

Fletcher, S (1992) *NVQs Standards and Competence*, London: Kogan Page.

HMSO (1975) *Sex Discrimination Act*, London: HMSO.

HMSO (1976) *Race Relations Act*, London: HMSO.

HMSO (1986) *Working Together, Education and Training*, Government White Paper, London: HMSO.

HMSO (1991) *Education and Training for the Twenty-first Century*, Government White Paper, London: HMSO.

HMSO (1994) *Competitiveness, Helping Business to Win*, Government White Paper, London: HMSO.

Hyland, T (1992) 'Meta-competence, metaphysics and vocational expertise', *Competence and Assessment*, 20, 22–24.

Handy, C (1990 *The Age of Unreason*, London: Arrow.

Jessup, G (1990) *Accreditation of Prior Learning in the Context of National Vocational Qualifications*, London: NCVQ.

Jessup, G (1991) *NVQs and the Emerging Model of Education and Training*, London: Falmer Press.

MSC (1981a) *A New Training Initiative: A Consultative Document*, Sheffield.

MSC (1981b) *A New Training Initiative: An Agenda for Action*, Sheffield.

MSC/NEDC (1986) *Review of Vocational Qualifications in England and Wales*, London: HMSO.

Mullin, R (1992) *Decisions and Judgements in NVQ-based Assessment*, London: NCVQ.

NCVQ (1993) *Awarding Bodies Common Accord*, London: NCVQ.

NCVQ (1994) *Implementing the National Standards for Assessment and Verification*, London: NCVQ.

NCVQ (1994) *Non-Discriminatory Assessment Practice*, London, NCVQ.

NCVQ (1995) *NVQ Criteria and Guidance*, London: NCVQ.

Papathomas, A (1990) *Open Access to Assessment for NVQs: New roles for the F E college*, London: NCVQ.

Rowntree, D (1987) *Assessing Students: How shall we know them?*, London: Kogan Page.

Simosko, S (1992) *APL: A practical guide for professionals*, London: Kogan Page.

Smithers, A (1993) *All Our Futures*, report commissioned for Channel 4 documentary.

TDLB (1992, revised 1994) *National Standards for Training and Development*, Crown Copyright, 1992/4.

Wolf, A (1993) *Assessment Issues and Problems in a Criterion-based System*, London: FEU.

Index